D1756525

THE
JUNGLE WAR
AGAINST THE JAPANESE

THE
JUNGLE WAR
AGAINST THE JAPANESE

FROM THE VETERANS FIGHTING IN ASIA, 1941–1945

TIM HEATH

PEN & SWORD
HISTORY

AN IMPRINT OF PEN & SWORD BOOKS LTD.
YORKSHIRE – PHILADELPHIA

To the memory of Colin & Brian Heath and David & Phillip Allsop

First published in Great Britain in 2021 by
PEN AND SWORD HISTORY
An imprint of
Pen & Sword Books Ltd
Yorkshire – Philadelphia

ISBN 978 1 52675 986 3

A CIP catalogue record for this book is available from the British Library.

Typeset in Times New Roman 11.5/14 by
SJmagic DESIGN SERVICES, India.
Printed and bound by CPI Group (UK) Ltd, Croydon, CR0 4YY

Pen & Sword Books Limited incorporates the imprints of Atlas, Archaeology,
Aviation, Discovery, Family History, Fiction, History, Maritime, Military,
Military Classics, Politics, Select, Transport, True Crime, Air World,
Frontline Publishing, Leo Cooper, Remember When, Seaforth Publishing,
The Praetorian Press, Wharncliffe Local History, Wharncliffe Transport,
Wharncliffe True Crime and White Owl.

For a complete list of Pen & Sword titles please contact
PEN & SWORD BOOKS LIMITED
47 Church Street, Barnsley, South Yorkshire, S70 2AS, England
E-mail: enquiries@pen-and-sword.co.uk
Website: www.pen-and-sword.co.uk

Or

PEN AND SWORD BOOKS
1950 Lawrence Rd, Havertown, PA 19083, USA
E-mail: Uspen-and-sword@casematepublishers.com
Website: www.penandswordbooks.com

Contents

Introduction

'As a young lad who joined up to become a soldier, I never imagined the horrors of war that were to come. I returned home not only a victorious Allied soldier, but also a man capable of killing without any remorse whatsoever. I hated them [the Japs] and I still do to this day.'

Carl Marksham, British Fourteenth
Army veteran, May 2010

On 8 December 1941 the British Empire, Canada and the Netherlands declared war on the Empire of Japan. The declaration of war was announced following Japanese attacks on British interests in Malaya, Singapore and Hong Kong. It was on that same date that the United States of America also issued their declaration of war against the Japanese. The surprise Japanese attack on the United States naval base at Pearl Harbor in Hawaii the previous morning heralded America's entry into the Second World War. China and Australia followed suit, issuing their declaration of war against Japan the next day. Four days later Germany and its Axis ally Italy both declared war against the United States.

For the British the United States's entry into the war could not have come soon enough. Although Britain was holding her own against the fury of the German Luftwaffe, it was perfectly clear to many that she could not defeat the might of Nazi Germany on her own. In this sense the Japanese attack on the United States could be seen today as a serious tactical blunder on the part of the Axis. The Japanese Empire had seriously underestimated both the resolve of the British combined with the industrial might of America. Although a long, difficult road to victory lay ahead for the Allies, both Britain and America were determined to destroy any dream of Japanese expansionism in Asia and the Pacific by combined military effort.

INTRODUCTION

The war against the Japanese, particularly in the dark, humid jungles of Asia and the Pacific, would be completely different from the one that was being fought against the Germans in Western Europe. It would be a war requiring a special form of courage, ingenuity and resolve in terrain often thought impossible to fight in by western standards. Initial British engagements with the Japanese forces in the jungles of Asia proved disastrous. Many British soldiers had convinced themselves that the jungle could not be mastered, that the Japanese had somehow become supermen overnight. Many were psychologically beaten before even engaging their Japanese enemy. The reality was that the jungle was just as harsh upon the Japanese as it was on anyone else. The major difference between British and Japanese soldiers was that the Japanese had learned to master the jungle in a way their British counterparts had not. The Japanese soldier was a greatly feared foe and for very good reason. The Japanese soldier was well equipped, and he was prepared to endure hardships that most Westerners would find intolerable, in order to secure victory for his Emperor. Bound by the warrior code of bushido, the Japanese soldier possessed a suicidal bravery in the face of even the most overwhelming odds. He would offer no surrender or ground to his enemy, preferring death to what he interpreted as dishonour. He possessed little to no compassion at all for his enemy and would kill with any means at his disposal. He could fight with a rifle, bayonet, knife or sword. He was a ruthless, brutal and unforgiving foe in every respect. As a result, the British forces tasked with fighting the Japanese enemy had to not only learn through bitter experience how to master the jungle but also how to effectively fight the Japanese who utilized the jungle to such cunning advantage. To the credit of the British, Indian, Nepalese, Australian and American forces engaged in dislodging the Japanese from their jungle strongholds, the lessons that would bring about victory were ultimately mastered. In turn, the Allied forces fighting the Japanese would also express little in the way of mercy toward their Asian enemy.

In this volume we will examine previously unpublished accounts of the jungle war against the Japanese in the Second World War. There are some events within the pages of this work that the reader may find too horrific to comprehend. The fact that human beings could be capable of such barbarity even in the name of war is sobering upon reflection. What is presented here is not only an analysis of how Allied ingenuity prevailed under difficult conditions to secure victory, a victory achieved over a particularly tenacious and barbarous enemy, but also the dividing line between the consciousness of the individual and how he conducts himself when faced with an enemy devoid of all human compassion.

Chapter 1

The Japanese: Origin of the Asian Enemy

From the moment the Second World War ended with the surrender of the Japanese, announced on 15 August 1945 and formally signed on 2 September 1945, historians have sought to understand the mentality behind the conduct of the Japanese military forces during the war. As an Asian race, the Japanese were of course different from westerners in cultural and religious perspectives, which is to be expected. Surely as fellow human beings they would have experienced much the same emotions, too? They would have lived, laughed, cried and mourned in much the same way as we in the western hemisphere despite the cultural and religious differences.

From the period known as the Meiji Restoration of 1868, under the Emperor Meiji the military began bringing to bear strong influence upon every aspect of Japanese society. Almost all leaders in Japanese society during this period were ex-Samurai or descendants of Samurai, all embracing the same outlook, principles and values. It was the influences of this early Meiji governing body that cultivated fear within the Japanese of Western imperialism and expansion. As a result of this paranoia, the Fukoku Kyohei – 'Enrich the country, strengthen the armed forces' – programme was instituted. It was brought about to strengthen the Japanese economy and industrial foundations in order for a strong and capable military force to be created. This in turn would be used to protect Japanese interests from outside influence.

Universal military conscription was introduced in 1873, enabling Japan's military to indoctrinate thousands of men from every conceivable background into the new military ideology. Patriotism and unquestioning loyalty to the Emperor were essential prerequisites. The Japanese were strongly influenced in their actions by the success of Prussia in transforming itself from a peasant state into that of a leading industrial-military power. Prussian political ideas based upon military expansion combined with authoritarian government at home were all adopted by the Japanese. Perhaps of greater importance was the adoption of a devalued civilian control in government over an independent military. This enabled the military to develop a state within a state, possessing greater political influence in general. Strongly influenced by the German victory in the Franco-Prussian War, the Japanese reacted with numerous recommendations for their military forces, including reorganization of the command structure of the army into divisions and regiments. This gave greater flexibility in improving strength, mobility and logistics and improving the overall transportation structure. All major bases of Japan's armed forces were connected by railroads. Artillery and engineering regiments were refined into independent commands. The Japanese also adopted the concept of war games to aid in the process not only of the training of individual soldiers but to sharpen the new military tactics adopted by the Japanese army. Subservience to the ruling Emperor was also of paramount importance. It was certainly no myth that the Japanese had been regarded as an inferior force in western minds. This was a theory which would not only be put to the test during the Second World War but was also quickly dispelled from western military thinking during the course of the war.

Conflict between China and Japan had existed for several years prior to the outbreak of the Second World War. Japanese barbarity had surfaced on many occasions during the course of the two Sino-Japanese wars. During the Second World War Japan had not been a signatory to the rules of the Geneva Convention of 27 July 1929. This version of the Geneva Convention was what governed the treatment of prisoners of war from the period 1939–1945. With this in mind it has to be said that the conduct of the Japanese military throughout the course of the First World War was at least comparable to that of the other belligerents. Why then was there such a departure from humanity in relation to the conduct of the Japanese military during the Second World War? To understand this, you have to firstly understand the Japanese military ethos of the day. Initially, the Japanese warrior code of bushido instilled a supposed distinctive set of qualities above those termed as the 'common rabble' of Japan. In its original context the Code of Bushido was an ideal originating from the Samurai, an ancient Japanese warrior order closely attached to Japan's nobility of medieval and early modern times. It was a philosophy adopted in an almost religious sense by Japan's military throughout the Second World War. It was a philosophy meant to emphasize honesty, filial piety, selflessness, honour, indifference to pain, obedience and total loyalty to one's superiors. It is obvious that the code of honour as associated with bushido was certainly transformed through Japan's imperial aspirations during the Second World War. Written in the early eighteenth century, a work titled *Hagakure* begins with the quotation: 'Bushido is a way of dying. Its basic thesis is that only a Samurai prepared and willing to die at any moment can devote himself entirely to his lord.' In the case of the Japanese soldier of the Second World War his life was to be gladly offered in the service to both country and Emperor. To die in this noble manner was considered as one of the greatest honours that could be bestowed. Of course, for the dead man such an honour was only in spirit yet for his family it carried with it great prestige. There was little in the way of mourning when the death of a young Japanese soldier was announced to his family back home. To have sacrificed his life for country and Emperor was considered the path to Nirvana. When many young men left their homes and families to begin their training prior to joining the Imperial Japanese Army, mothers and fathers never expected their sons to return home again. It was a completely alien outlook to that of the families of British, American, Indian and Australian servicemen. The understanding of this basic principle of Japanese military thinking is vital in grasping why many Japanese soldiers behaved in the manner they did throughout the war. This by no means offers any excuses for Japanese barbarity for which they soon became notorious. Yet it does emphasize how the original Japanese Code of Bushido was distorted to suit their imperialist desires of the Second World War.

The Japanese military's reputation for barbarity had already been cemented with the Nanking Massacre also referred to as the Rape of Nanking. This incident, which took place over a period of six weeks from 13 December 1937 (the day that the Japanese captured Nanking) to January 1938, was an atrocity which shocked the civilized world. The unfortunate victims of this orgy of rape and murder were the residents of Nanking, the capital of China, during the Second Sino-Japanese War. The population of Nanking was subjected to unspeakable horrors, some so disgusting that many historians have declined to publish the details.

The death toll among Chinese civilians and disarmed combatants has been quoted at 40,000 to 300,000. Due to the fact that many military records on the incident were destroyed or kept secret by the Japanese authorities after the surrender of Japan in 1945, it has been difficult to ascertain the true scale of the massacre. To this day it is the subject of much debate among scholars and historians. To those who witnessed and survived the Nanking Massacre it was an event that even today remains a running sore in the memory.

Chi Wong was just a child of 8 when the Japanese entered Nanking. She was home with her mother, father and grandmother at the time. They had locked the door to their home and were hiding in what she described as an alcove within the small wooden building. Chi had never spoken of her ordeal and asked that her grandson provide the following account for this volume. Chi's grandson, Huang Fu Jian, who now lives in the US, recalled: 'My grandmother remembers it very clearly in her mind and she said':

I was in hiding with my mother, father and grandmother when the Japanese troops came. The Japanese could be clearly heard outside the house. There was the constant sound of rifle fire and they were shouting very loudly. They had been working their way up through the streets kicking in the doors to the houses. They would kick down doors, throw grenades into the houses and rush in with their bayonets to finish off any survivors inside. There was no opposition to them and when they got to our home, they kicked down the door, fired a few wild shots into the house and began to search the house room by room. We heard crashing noises as they kicked furnishings over and began searching for anything of value. We had no valuables as we were just simple people.

They found our hiding place and immediately they pointed their rifles at us and began to shout waving for us to come outside. They had these long bayonets on the ends of their rifles, I recall one dripping with blood. My grandmother's legs were not quick enough, so they kicked her full force in the back. The force of the kick sent my grandmother to the floor where she hit her face against the ground. My mother went to help her up when she was kicked in the stomach. I remember my mother lying on the ground where the Japanese continued to kick her. She cried out but they wouldn't stop kicking her. My grandmother lay motionless and a pool of blood began to form around her head.

My father and I were pushed outside. One of the Japanese began removing my mother's clothing. They stripped her clothes off and one by one they raped my mother, forcing my father to watch at rifle point. My mother was repeatedly slapped and punched during the rape. When they finished with her, they put their knives [bayonets] in her. I know that one of the Japanese forced his knife into my mother's abdomen through her vaginal orifice. Both my mother and grandmother were repeatedly stabbed by the soldiers. They did all these things while showing us no mercy at all and their faces were filled with hate and anger. My father was hysterical, crying and pleading 'mercy, mercy' with them. I was in a state of shock; I felt numb and unable to cry out. My father continued to plead with the Japanese. He wanted them to leave us; they did leave but before leaving us they shot my father in the head with a pistol. My father fell dead at my side.

They then turned their attention to me. Speaking Chinese, they called me a 'pig', a 'Chinese whore'. I was just a child, yet they showed me no pity. They stripped me naked and one of them held me and put out his cigarette on my chest. The others stood there laughing as he did this to me. Then one of them pushed me down and sat on me trying to force his penis into my mouth. He was shouting something like 'nice you suck now' and 'you no bite or this' and he held a knife to my throat. It made me choke as I could not breathe. I was terrified of hurting him and giving him the excuse to slice open my throat. As he did this to me, I could feel the fingers of the other soldiers between my legs. All the time they were laughing and shouting to each other as if it were some kind of game. The pain of what the other soldiers were doing to me was excruciating. It felt as if he were pushing something up inside me. When the one on top of me finished, he slapped me several times to the point where I must have lost consciousness.

I was later found in another room wrapped up in a sheet. It was one of the neighbours of ours who found me, and she took me into her home. She was naked from the waist up herself. She was covered in cuts and bruises and had been violated. I remained in her care until my uncle came for me some weeks later.

My uncle forbade me to ever talk about what happened to anyone. He would insist, 'You say nothing as you must preserve yours and our respect. If anyone hears of this, they will never want to touch you.' He was referring to me marrying and what any future husband might think. So, I was told to stay silent all these years. For years I have had to cry within myself, unable to tell anyone. I want the world to know my story of what the Japanese did to us. We were human beings; we did no wrong to any Japanese other than being Chinese; we had done no one any wrong. Why did they hate us so much and enjoy inflicting so much pain on us and others? I don't know as only they who did these terrible things can know the answers.

Chi's story is typical of the many Chinese survivors of the Nanking Massacre. The barbaric practices of the Imperial Japanese Army would be repeated everywhere they went during their period of conquest in the Second World War. Of the Nanking Massacre, former Japanese soldier Akihara Koto said:

I was not serving in the Japanese army when our forces went into Nanking, yet my belief in our philosophy regarding our enemies and how we should deal with them was already instilled within me. I knew it was a matter of both time and honour that I should join the army. We in Japan just felt that this was our time, our rising as the sun would rise each morning. How our soldiers dealt with the Chinese was of no concern to our society, as we felt at that time that they were below us and we held them in contempt. This may be difficult for western minds to understand but we had no feelings of pity towards our enemy at all. Those that gave up without a fight were regarded as the lowest of the low. If any soldiers gave up while engaged in fighting with us Japanese, it displayed a lack of courage and a lack of honour in our view of things. Such people were not worthy of life as by way of cowardice they had lost all right to that gift that is life. We were schooled in the thought that one should never give up even when faced with the greatest of odds against survival. To die a warrior was the greatest honour both for the soldier and his family back home. The family of course would have a sense of loss but the sense of pride in their son carrying out his ultimate duty outweighed the feelings of sorrow. They would all meet again in the great nirvana; that is how many young Japanese men were educated. It was all about an individual and his honour and that he should not bring disgrace to his country or his family. If he was chosen to die, then he should go to his death with glory. For the Japanese soldier this was the only way it could be, and this is how we differed from the soldiers of other nations such as the British Empire and the United States of America. How could any warrior disgrace himself by being taken prisoner? Such a man in our thinking was not a warrior but a coward unworthy of life.

The Japanese possessed a rabid hatred of the European colonists in South-East Asia who in the inter-wars period felt that their empires were secure. The British, French and Dutch had all played a part in transplanting a European lifestyle in Asia. Grand mansions were built, their bleached white stone often appearing out of place within the environment around them. Locals were of course employed as either workers or servants for these wealthy colonials. It is no surprise that both despised one another with equal measure. The British regarded the indigenous peoples as sub-human, lacking in intellect, unworthy of the same levels of respect as themselves. In the opulent clubs and bars that came about through white European domination, only whites were permitted entry.

The Dutch colonials were less aloof than the British and French. They proved to be heavy drinkers, particularly of gin and beer, they adopted some of the local traditional dress as worn by the locals and fraternized freely with the natives. Many Dutch males took native wives and single Dutch men enjoyed relationships with native women as a matter of course. As employers the Dutch were regarded as harsh, driving their workers relentlessly and paying them little – four cents a day being the average. The Dutch appeared totally ignorant to the new nationalist threat growing in their midst; when the end came, it would not only come as a complete shock but a battle for survival too.

The Asians marvelled at the luxury of the Europeans with their fine clothes, afternoon teas, tennis courts, cricket matches and golf courses. When the colonial dream came crashing down, it was simple for the Japanese to convince the indigenous peoples to turn against their 'white masters' who had exploited them essentially as slaves and join what the Japanese had termed the Asian Co-prosperity Sphere.

Chapter 2

A Desire for War

The Imperial Japanese Army – the IJA – or Army of the Greater Japanese Empire was the official ground-based armed force of the Japanese Empire from 1868 to 1945. Although control came under the auspices of the Imperial Japanese Army General Staff Office and the Ministry of the Army, both were in effect subordinate to the Emperor of Japan. The Emperor in question for this period of study was Emperor Hirohito. At the start of Hirohito's reign, Japan was already establishing itself as one of the world's great powers, boasting the ninth-largest economy in the world, the third-largest navy and one of the four permanent members of the League of Nations. The Emperor himself was greatly revered by Japanese society who worshipped him as if he were a living deity. Hirohito was also supreme commander of the Japanese army and naval forces and, had the will been there, he could have intervened and checked the aggressive military ambitions of his armed forces. In this context there can be no excuses on Hirohito's part: he was every bit a war criminal as the Japanese soldiers who raped and murdered their way across China prior to the Second World War and through Asia and the Pacific throughout the war. The fact that Hirohito would remain as emperor of the Japanese people after 1945 and face no punishment for the conduct of the Japanese military forces has been a source of great bitterness among British veterans of the war in Asia ever since.

From 1934 it was clear that Japan was increasing its military strength, yet the world appeared unconcerned. By 1941 the IJA had at its disposal fifty-one divisions combined with a variety of special-purpose artillery, cavalry, anti-aircraft and armoured units comprising a total of 1,700,000 troops. Although often derided as being nothing more than 'monkeys' by much of the western world, particularly the wealthy white colonialists sipping cocktails on the verandas of their estates, the Japanese were very eager to flex their muscles and prove they possessed a far greater ingenuity than what their white enemies could have ever given them credit for. The Japanese soldier himself was well equipped for the task he was about to embark upon.

Akihara Koto recalls what military training was like for an ordinary Japanese soldier:

> Those of us who were the pre-Second World War soldiers underwent very extensive military training within the army. It was my family's desire that I become a soldier and serve our Emperor. I had cast aside any notions of going on to study until I had completed at least some service with our army. It was clear even to us lower ranks that something was going to happen, that something big was being planned, and that we would be playing a vital part.
>
> The training was incredibly harsh and the training back then for recruits took place over a period of one year. There was no room at all for weaklings, and weakling recruits were subjected to far more brutal treatment than the stronger ones; that was the nature of it back then. The first months of training were mainly concerned with the basic principles of soldiering. As a soldier, the moment you entered the ranks of the army you were the property of the army itself. I was issued with a uniform and much of the early training was based on physical fitness, training with bayonets, basic marksmanship, field training and platoon and company training and exercises. Every step of the way they would try to break you and beatings were frequent.
>
> We also had to be able to march twenty miles a day towards the end of our training programme. The fitness regime was therefore extremely thorough, and we had to be able to carry out rifle drill and strip and reassemble our weapons within a specified time. I know one young man who failed a couple of times; the sergeant in charge of us beat him over the head with a Kendo stick he always carried. There were many times where the sergeants and other higher ranks would kick, beat and slap you for nothing. If you ever forgot to bow to the higher-ranking soldiers, you would be savagely beaten. They would deprive us of

food and water and have us stand to attention for very long periods of time. If a man dared fall, he would be beaten and shouted at. They would shout, 'You are a disgrace and not worthy of the skin you are wearing.' Yes, they beat, slapped and kicked us with their bare hands, sticks and even rifles. They filled us with hatred, yet the hatred they told us should be directed towards the westerners in our midst, not those who were actually beating us who were of course our own superiors. The sergeant given charge of us told us, 'You do not cry, you do not feel any pain, you do not show any mercy, you do not show any cowardice and you should be prepared to die at any moment for country, family and Emperor.' To display to us young men what he meant he began to remove his shirt to reveal his bare torso. He looked strong and well defined, the perspiration on his skin seemed to accentuate his muscularity as the light from the sun beat down upon him. He then handed his Kendo stick to a Corporal Tashiwara and instructed the corporal to deliver a full-force blow with the stick across the middle of his back. We watched in disbelief as the corporal carried out the sergeant's wish. I blinked momentarily as the stick cracked as it made contact with the sergeant's back. He stood rooted to the spot with his hands placed upon his head and he showed no sense of pain and did not flinch for one instant. He ordered the corporal to hit him three more times to show us that pain and suffering were something in the mind, something through the practising of Bushido that could be overcome, that a man's pain could be destroyed and taken out of his mind and physical being altogether. After this we were told that we would have to bear the same pain if we were to succeed. The sergeant then said to us, 'A man who can shoulder and bear the greatest of pain, and relinquish all sense of pity for his enemies is the man who will conquer the world.' We stood listening to him and we wcrc all sweating profusely more from nervousness than the heat. The sergeant began walking up and down examining us, looking deep into our eyes. He stood and momentarily glared into my eyes. I'd never seen eyes like his before; they were cold, steel, unrelenting as if a storm was somehow captured and residing deep within them. Yet at the same time I wished I could be him, as brave and noble as he was. He then dismissed us from the day's duty, and we were ordered to our simple wooden hut quarters.

Even when dismissed from duty we were constantly harassed and called to attention. The sergeant would enter the hut and whatever we were doing we would have to stop and we would jump up to attention. He would walk about the hut inspecting everything and if something displeased him, he would burst into a rage and slap us all one by one. The regime became increasingly brutal so much so that some men began to break before his eyes, to question their own sanity. One broke down and fell to his knees and the sergeant shouted at him, 'You are no good for the army of the Empire of Japan, you are only good for looking after prisoners like a woman.' We never saw that young man again; I don't know if he was sent to do other war work. Either way, accepting defeat was not the thing to do, not in our army it wasn't.

The next day we were lectured on how rice was our divine food sent by the gods so the Japanese people would never starve. Of course, we all understood the value placed upon the diet of rice which we all ate. We were all raised on rice as part of our traditional diet and yes, it was considered sacred in every true Japanese household. I recall the one day we were told we would have to learn to march on just two rice balls per day; some conditions in the field of combat might dictate this action someday, we were told. We were not happy about this, but we gritted our teeth and we did as we were told and for a few days we ate only two rice balls yet carried out the same hard physical training of running up and down hills and rifle drill with full combat order. We also carried out much night-time battle training. Night was always a good time to attack an enemy especially in a jungle environment. After the few days had passed, we were given a banquet of rice with fish and rice with pork as a reward.

I found the rifle training very good; the Arisaka rifle was simple to use and maintain and when we began shooting training, I could say I was a good shot. The basic marksmanship of other men in our unit varied considerably from good to excellent. Our sergeant told us that 'white men think we have bad eyes, that we Japanese cannot see as well as what they do, and we cannot shoot as accurately as what they do. Well, we will show them.' The few who shot poorly were of course punished for not paying attention in the usual manner. They would receive a slap across the face and told 'do it again, shoot until you can shoot properly'. There was no getting away from it and if you were beaten up it soon became an incentive to do the best you could.

There was a lot of emphasis on bayonet fighting which required great individual courage, we were told. A heavy sack would be strung up from a tree and we would have to put in a mock charge screaming as we did so and thrust the bayonet into the sack as if it were an enemy soldier. The sergeant was not happy with stabbing grain or rice bags filled with sand or straw so he brought us along a live goat once so as we could actually see some blood. The goat was strung up by both of its back legs; it tried to struggle and made much noise as it was hung up from the tree. The sergeant became annoyed and struck the goat a blow with his fist. He told us, 'Even a goat must respect me!' Yet the animal continued to cry out. One by one we were told to charge the goat with our bayonets. The animal was still struggling and making noises even after being stabbed and partially disembowelled by the third man. Then it was my turn. I pointed my rifle and charged, yelling what would become a traditional war cry: '*Banzai!*' I thrust the blade of the bayonet into the goat's body which then began to twitch. I returned and stood back in line proud that I had done this, then the next man ran forward with his bayonet but by this time I think the goat had died. He thrust the bayonet into the goat's abdomen, and I watched as the entrails spilled from the hole made by our blades. We were ordered again and again to repeat our attacks on the goat carcass before the sergeant was happy. By the time the sergeant was satisfied the goat was barely recognizable. He unsheathed the sword he carried with him, carefully lined it up with the centre of the animal's abdomen and with a *swish* he cut it in half. We were told we could eat the meat from the animal We were ordered to line up to attention once again and then to clean our bayonets of the goat's blood and entrails. We then had some food and water before having to line up again.

Some other soldiers came in a vehicle and pulled a man from out of the back of the vehicle. The man was tanned and of local native origin although I am not sure. There was a lot of commotion. He was blindfolded and his hands were tied tightly behind his back. He was pushed up with his back against the tree that the goat had previously been hanging from. We looked at one another as we guessed what was coming, yet we felt excitement at the prospect of killing a live human being with our bayonets. An officer had explained that the man had been caught stealing rice from the Japanese and that death was the only way that such a lowly individual might redeem himself having stolen property of the Japanese Empire. The man made no cries for mercy nor showed any emotion from what we could see of his face, yet I watched as he uttered something with his lips, I could see them moving. Then, again, one by one, we each took a turn with our bayonets. I watched as the first man thrust forward, there was a curious crunching sound like bones being broken; the man's head slumped down, his chin resting on his chest and I guessed he had been killed with the first thrust. I watched the soldier as he thrust several times into the heart before returning to the line. When it came to my turn the man's body was drenched in blood and I could clearly see the entry wounds made by our blades. Did I feel anything for this man described as a thief? No, I felt nothing at all and if any man were to steal rice from my people then I would feel that this course of action would be the only justice.

Later that day the goat carcass was cooked as a special treat for all of us soldiers. We then sat in our hut and rejoiced.

We understood that soon we might be at war; we felt as Japanese we had little choice. Some of the British had called us 'the yellow men with poor eyesight and glasses' and the wealthy white colonials had called us 'monkeys'. They felt we were inferior to them, like lowly natives who served them and worked for them. War was not guaranteed at that point, yet many of us yearned for it. I wanted to meet these white imperialists in combat and show them I was no yellow man and I was no ape. There was much talk of eliminating the white enemy from the whole of Asia and creating a prosperity not built upon white imperial ideals but Asian and Japanese ideals. I believe many Asians greeted this idea but were unsure if it could ever be a success. Our task was to make it a success for our peoples to work together as Asians.

As our training regime continued the military exercises we were set to accomplish grew in importance. We began to carry out increased levels of night-time training, the marches became longer and combined exercises at regimental and battalion levels were carried out. There was also a great deal of classroom work. Like children would sit at their desks in school, we were schooled in obstacle clearing, the identification of certain sounds both at night and in daytime, camouflage and concealment, map and compass reading and patrol and security detail. The training was very comprehensive and the fact that a large number of our army saw action in Manchuria prior to the war meant that much valuable military experience had been gained and could be passed on to new soldiers. Experience is everything; practice and training help but nothing compares to having been in combat when you are planning for a future war.

We were also spiritually prepared for every endeavour which lay ahead of us in our lives as Japanese soldiers. We practised spirituality as did the ancient Samurai along with the ancient Bushido code of the warrior. I recall a visit to what was a very important shrine to the Japanese military at Yasakuni. This shrine contained the names of Japanese soldiers who had died in the service of their country.

We were told if we did the same and died for our country, far from being forgotten, we would be remembered as heroes like here at this shrine. Our country would never allow any individual sacrifice to become blurred and lost within the mists of our history. It was a comforting thought and I felt calm that if I should die in battle, not only would I too reach the very heights of spirituality as a spiritual warrior but generations later I would still be remembered. I felt that I understood the violence from which we as recruits had been wrought. I understood that violence was the only way to ensure we became strong both physically and mentally; by no other means could we have achieved that level of preparedness as soldiers. Those who couldn't succeed for whatever reason were consigned to the tasks of natives, things like sweeping our streets, catching rats and worst of all begging from the wealthy with a bowl. That was in my opinion a fate worse than death.

People are curious as to why so much emphasis was placed upon the use of the bayonet in the Japanese military. The answer is simple and yet again lies with the ancient Samurai warrior tradition. To use a piece of steel in combat and take an enemy's life with that piece of steel was viewed as the ultimate expression of our warrior code and tradition. It was once said to us that the fixing of the bayonet to the end of your rifle is more than just an action, or a simple message of intent towards your foe in battle; that piece of steel becomes a piece of your soul, it is you, it is in your soul at that point in time. The soldier who then kills with either his bayonet or sword [if he carries one] is then the ultimate personification of the ancient Samurai warrior who dispatched his enemies in the same way centuries earlier. The use of the bayonet was not seen as a barbaric action to us; quite the contrary: to use the bayonet was the ultimate honour and expression of a man's bravery, as it was easier to shoot a bullet, but bullets require no courage to shoot. In comparison, the bayonet requires great personal courage, as you must take the ground from beneath your enemy's boots, get to grips with him physically and with all your force you then must kill him. If you succeed you have expressed your bravery as required by the code of the Samurai, and you have proved yourself worthy in that context.

It was a military discipline that I know was alien to our westernized enemies. They too trained with bayonets but were they as eager to use them as what we were? No, I don't think they were, not at first anyway. Even with a knife we were trained to be just as tenacious. We were trained in a way that many special forces would later be trained. To use stealth and concealment, to stalk an enemy, appear from nowhere, stab him and then disappear back into the darkness. Such actions against an enemy would have a great effect upon their morale: it would be a great psychological blow.

All of this you may say adds up to the actions of an uneducated enemy; well, you would be wrong again. Our classroom work as we called it was devised to erase illiteracy, to educate us to a high standard. We learned mathematics, science, physics and geography. Military tactical thinking was also taught which covered most battlefield scenarios. Languages were also studied very closely along with the various methods of signals and communications, not only those used by our army but also that of nations we might one day face in battle. We studied in detail the cultures and traditions of the British during our training. We understood the British were an aloof nation yet proud also. They were an empire that had used aggression throughout its existence and as a result benefited from enslaving natives along the way. India was one of the primary examples of this and we studied the thinking behind it all.

The Japanese could never allow themselves to become slaves in this manner; it was a sign of weakness to accept a life of slavery rather than fight to the death for freedom and in defence of one's culture and tradition. Anything else was totally unacceptable in Japanese military thinking. Therefore, cowardice and surrender were viewed as an obscenity in our eyes. Both would invite dishonour and shame upon a family. The classroom work also dictated to us that the best means of preventing the spread of the wealthy colonialists and their empire was a decisive first strike where aggression, speed and mercilessness were the vital elements. It all made sense to me and my army friends at that time. We feared the spread of the white colonial powers. We knew of their own barbarity and how they had gained their power and wealth; we knew how they treated their native servants who were not even treated on the same level as the pet dogs: the dogs lived in better conditions and ate better too. I remember becoming very angry when I thought about it all.

The classroom work really instilled that sense of preparedness within me, I thought, 'How did these people manage to do this, and why did the races ensnared within their grasp just tolerate the existence they were given?' Such people were merely existing upon the charity of these wealthy aristocratic westerners who held them in higher contempt than a dog. All these factors encouraged me and those soldiers with me to train ever harder, to push ourselves to the limits of what we could tolerate. I had never even met a westerner prior to the war, but I hated them so much and I prayed that I would have my chance to fight them in battle.

During the course of our training it was even permitted that if we found ourselves in a survival life or death situation that we could even use the corpses of our enemy to survive. We understood that meant the unthinkable in the eyes of many, eating the meat of slain enemies. Yes, one might question as to whether or not such an action might be ethical, that one might be cursed for eating the flesh of a fellow human being. We were taught simply that this was a sentimental notion that westerners adhered to, that it was in bad taste, that you did not do this under any circumstances, that there would be moral consequences for such actions. As we did not share the same beliefs as the westerners and lived by an entirely different code in the military sense, we felt if the time came, we would do it. If faced with the choice of eating my enemy or slowly starving to death, then I would see no problem with doing the former. I couldn't see how such an action would make me a beast. Why is the killing and consumption of an animal any less barbaric than that of a human? An animal feels pain, it lives, it breathes, it has emotions and feelings, yet humanity disregards these factors as nonsense, that only we as human beings have the rights to breathe, feel no pain and be treated in accordance with the rules of the great creator. I have never understood this way of thinking, which is probably why I have always valued the lives of animals and other small creatures. In my opinion animals are the purest things on earth after water; they don't kill for pleasure or in the name of conquest as do human beings.

So, now you may be thinking I am a very philosophical man, quite apart from how you were thinking I would be. In a sense I did what I had to do in the service of my country, I was not a hypocrite, I lived a humble existence, and I did not yearn for wealth at the expense of my fellow man. These were simple lessons taught to me by my father, despite what many historians think and write about us today; some of us were deeply spiritual people.

By the time my call to action came, I felt I was more than ready to meet the challenges that would be thrown in my path. I knew it would not all be pleasant, that I would see many horrors, that I would have to kill without mercy, but I had accepted these things; my training had instilled the military values and discipline necessary to carry out my tasks. My family were overjoyed at seeing their son become a trained soldier; we posed for portrait photographs. I would stand with my father and mother in my uniform while they both wore traditional dress. Then my sister would have her photograph taken standing with me. The pride in my sister's face was beyond words; we had always got on very well unlike many siblings. I vowed I would protect not only the values, traditions and customs of Japan, but also those of my dearest family. If it meant laying down my life for them, then I was more than prepared to do this. Westerners in comparison didn't want to die; they talked of nothing more than going home, which is why we were such a formidable and fearsome enemy. My family did not expect me to return home; they had already come to terms with that basic philosophy and were at total peace with it all.

The officer class of the Japanese military was trained and educated in an even harsher environment than the lower ranks. NCOs too were subjected to even more violence and brutality in training from their superiors than the lower-ranking soldiers. Whatever a lower-ranking soldier could tolerate, an NCO had to be able to suffer double. All in a sense were treated as equals; the Japanese military was one which defied the hierarchic structures that most modern armies of the day favoured. For example, the Japanese Special Naval Landing Forces trained as infantry, whereas in the United States their naval landing forces were known as marines. The Japanese naval landing forces never adopted the title of marines, as they were never considered elite in Japanese military thinking. Japanese officers were expected to carry out hours of study outside the military academies, They had to maintain a high state of physical fitness and readiness for combat. Any officer who lagged in any of the required attributes of a Japanese officer would be subjected to the same rigorous discipline as the lowest of ranks, including face slapping which was commonplace throughout the Japanese military and was viewed as a humiliation that few wished to be subjected to.

Akihara Koto himself felt the humiliation of face slapping on more than one occasion during his yearlong training. If one of his friends was set a task and made an error in carrying out that task, then every man in the company would be punished. He recalls:

> There was an occasion one of the men in our company had failed to clean his weapon in the correct manner. When the commanding officer carried out his inspection, he was furious and began shouting and he ordered the sergeant to slap the face of every man in the company. So, he started at the top of the line and worked his way down it. Each man had a full-force slap across his face as a punishment. We were all given extra PT and rifle drill, and to round it all off we had to go on a five-mile run and lose all our privileges for two days. It was very severe but then going into action with a rifle which might not function correctly due to dirt

or other things would be even worse, so it could not be tolerated. That was how it was, and soldiers who shirked or were lazy in their duties were punished and if one messed up, we all messed up in the eyes of the commanding officer. We were all angry at the man causing us such humiliation that later when we were all alone, he was threatened; we told him, 'You do anything like that again and you will have a beating from all of us.' It did the trick as he never did anything like it again. I heard many such stories including one where men who made serious mistakes in training were actually whipped. I did not witness anything like that myself but those who told me about these things were honest individuals whom I knew would never have lied about such events.

Another thing I recall were the rewards we received for our dedication and good work in our training. The one evening some girls were brought to our barracks. They were very pretty Japanese girls who we were told were to be our reward for exemplary conduct. We could not believe our luck, and as many of us had not been with a woman since starting our military life, we were all like kids in a candy shop. We were made to wait though as the commanding officer gave a little speech to us. The girls just stood there in their pretty dresses looking at us and smiling. When the commanding officer had finished his speech, we gave him a bow and he bowed to us then stepped aside and the girls lined up in front of us. We had to take the girl who stood in front of us; there could be no negotiation, it was just like that. They were all very beautiful, so I didn't mind at all. I did not fancy having a company of other soldiers all watching me with this girl, so we went off for a walk and some privacy. We were allowed just one night with the girls and they would leave the barracks the next morning. We could even swap them if we so desired, and I had another two girls before dawn next day. We were even each issued with a handful of contraceptives, though I know some of the men did not use them. I recall one of my friends having a bit of a scare some days later. He came to me for advice and was very concerned; he told me that his genitals were itching badly, and he thought he might have contracted a sexual disease from one of the girls. I could not help him as I would not have known what a sexual disease looked like. He was so scared that he dropped his trousers and underwear and showed me his genitals. They were red from scratching and small blisters were visible on and around his penis. It looked horrible and I told him, 'Look, you had better go and see the medical officer this instant,' which he did and yes it was confirmed that he had contracted something from one of the girls. He was given medication and it cleared up after a relatively short period of time. After that incident, we were all lectured on cleanliness and were told that in future we must use the contraceptives provided to us, that there were health risks with ignoring the warnings. Despite the reward of the previous evening, we were still expected to carry out our allotted duties the following morning, starting with a parade and bowing to our flag. Most of us were very tired from the evening's antics, but we were also very happy with ourselves – like dogs with bones as they say.

When asked as to why the Imperial Japanese Army proved so effective in jungle warfare when compared to their western enemies, Akihara Koto's response was hardly surprising:

Fighting in the jungle is all about prior preparation and a comprehensive understanding of both your own limitations and those of your enemy, and what influences certain factors are going to have upon your tactical planning. For example, we understood the environment over which we would be fighting. Tactically, we were trained to utilize the environment to our advantage. Some jungle terrain we fought over was similar to that back home in Japan, with a similar climate in some regions, so it was not that alien to us as it may have been to a British or American soldier who had only ever experienced life in an urban concrete environment.

The basic rule for fighting an enemy in the jungle is that if you plan to attack an enemy position, the best times to attack are dawn or dusk. Jungles are often dark by their very nature so the darker it is the better chance your attack has of succeeding. Attack during the darkest times of dusk, nightfall and dawn has a very disorientating effect on an enemy. If it was raining, then this was considered even better as opposed to being a hinderance to us. The noise of rain falling on the jungle canopy has the effect of masking any noise of your approach. The British had the habit of going under tents or down into their trenches when it rained, which made it easier for us to take them by surprise. Did they not think about this? Did they not think that this would be the best time to attack them? We used to laugh at their incompetence and their attitude to things like the rain. All our orders were memorized and never written down on paper. This was something we had to learn early in our training, to memorize everything and never make notes which could then fall into enemy hands.

We were trained that it was not a good idea to concentrate your attack on the enemy's frontal force, that we should also concentrate on attacking the enemy's rear and flanks. If we were compromised by our enemy as we approached, we were instructed to remain still and quiet and not return fire; the commanding officer would assess the situation and then give orders on how the attack should proceed.

We were always to be vigilant for enemy booby traps, trip wires, observers and snipers. It was normal for pathfinders to be ahead of us, specifically looking to detect booby traps and tripwires or flares. The enemy used to string these out around their dug-in positions to give early warning of an attack. We relied on hand signals, yet sometimes it was so dark that if a trap was found you had to tap the man behind you and gesture for him to relay back that danger had been found. A tripwire was dealt with by lying on top of it and allowing your fellow soldiers to walk or crawl over you.

We would have artillery support due to the limited fields of fire; heavy weapons would be used to bombard an enemy defensive position then we would move up behind the artillery before launching our attack on the front, rear and flanks. Often the enemy began to fire wildly into the darkness as soon as our artillery opened fire. This made it easier for us to direct the artillery shells onto their positions.

Once the attack went in, we were to press home with it and should never retreat unless commanded to do so by our officers. We had mortar and machine-gun cover during the assault and the rest was up to us as individuals yet fighting as a well-coordinated force. We also had to understand the fact that if badly wounded we would have to be left behind if our troops were unable to get to us or were beaten back by the enemy. Our forces would of course try to retrieve us later if possible. If captured by the enemy due to wounds, we were told to always keep our weapons with us. We should fire on the enemy until the point came where we would end our own lives rather than fall into enemy captivity. Yes, we would kill ourselves rather than be captured and interrogated. The best way to kill yourself if wounded and facing capture was to use a sidearm. Place the barrel in your mouth until the muzzle of the pistol is firmly against the roof of the mouth in the centre. When the trigger is squeezed the bullet will destroy the brain in an instant. Some of us carried knives and these could also be used as a means of suicide before capture. We were schooled in these techniques: you feel the ribcage in front of the heart; you feel this when you press your fingers into the skin in this area. Then you place the blade point between the two bones before the heart and thrust with all your remaining strength. The blade would go right through the heart with no problem and death would be instant. These blades would be sharpened constantly for use against the enemy or to take our own lives if there were no other means. The blades were so sharp you could use them to shave with of a morning.

These were the basic principles which had to be learned thoroughly. Ritual suicide was another method, but this required a second man. While you disembowelled yourself with a shortened sword or knife, the other man would remove your head simultaneously with his sword. Many Japanese soldiers chose this method rather than be taken alive like a coward.

Akihara Koto's narrative surprised me somewhat. As I read through his first draft, which had transpired as the result of some lengthy journalistic interrogation, I was indeed surprised to discover that far from the cryptic ramblings of some mindless brute, I was actually corresponding with a man who was not only quite articulate, but deeply philosophical regarding his position in life and the world about him. How would I connect this spiritual and philosophical man in the context of the events which would later occur? Often the greatest challenge facing any military historian is that of remaining impartial while endeavouring to gain all the necessary facts. Time and again throughout this work I would find this a struggle.

Chapter 3

Law of the Jungle

The jungle has and always will remain a neutral entity to those armies who find themselves waging wars within its dark, humid and somewhat mysterious recesses. The jungle is a unique environment which in times of war favours neither friend nor foe, but rather those who adapt to the unique conditions which present themselves in jungle warfare. Western armies have an inherent urbanized psyche and have subsequently never really coped well in jungle environments, The reasons for this are many and varied. There are firstly many psychological factors that come into play. I remember as a child the stories of jungle exploration where pack-laden westerners sweating profusely would hack their way noisily through a maze of endless foliage, concealing all manner of deadly threats which included spiders, scorpions and snakes, often while being stalked in the near-impenetrable gloom by natives armed with poison darts. Such scenarios were of course a high degree of fiction laced with some degree of truth. It is with this image in mind that many of the soldiers of western nations entered into the jungle environment during the Second World War. In many cases they were psychologically beaten before even entering the jungle. The positive mental attitude required to operate in jungle terrain just wasn't there during the early phases of the war in Asia against the Japanese. At that time the nearest the British soldier had come to being within a jungle environment was if he had been garrisoned in India and had seen service there, though this was hardly in the same context as fighting a brutal war against an unforgiving enemy who had prepared well to fight in such difficult and alien terrain.

It is not difficult to then believe that some soldiers have died quite inexplicably at the prospect of having to enter the jungle. There was a case post-Second World War where a young man was about to undertake jungle warfare survival training with his platoon. The man had collapsed and died before he was even out of earshot of the traffic of a nearby city.

No plausible medical explanation could be determined for the cause of his sudden expiry other than the total fear he had felt prior to entering the jungle for his training – he had by all accounts died of fright. There were during the Second World War numerous accounts of men deliberately injuring themselves to prevent their selection for a jungle patrol, such was the fear of the jungle. Breaking down this irrational fear as it was viewed by the British command in the Second World War would not be a rapid or simple process.

In this chapter we will examine some of the aspects of the jungle environment that both British and Japanese soldiers found themselves confronted with, aspects such as the terrain, climate and natural hazards that presented themselves on a daily basis. Yes, jungle warfare requires many personal adaptations of a fighting man, yet so does arctic, desert and urban warfare. Jungle warfare has occurred frequently over the centuries and is as old as man's desire for conquest itself. Countries that have experienced fighting within their jungles include Burma, north-east India, Malay(si)a, Indonesia, Borneo, Laos, Vietnam and Thailand and of course the islands of the western Pacific – particularly the Philippine Islands and New Guinea. Jungle terrain ranges from dense, near-impenetrable tropical forest to patches of open spaces. The common problems facing any army within a jungle environment are those of limited visibility which affect both ground and air forces, and the lack of suitable tracks and/or roads which subsequently have an effect on both vehicle and troop mobility. Where jungle roads are available there will be certain times of the year where these roads may become impassable due to flood or monsoon conditions which prevail in the tropics. It was soon discovered that large vehicles generally coped well on jungle roads throughout the dry seasons, yet when the monsoon rains arrived, they soon sank axle-deep in the mud which had rapidly formed. The efforts in extricating vehicles from the resulting quagmire was extremely demanding and physically exhausting. British soldier Thomas 'Tommie' Watkins recalled:

> The monsoon season was one of the most dreaded of things. It would be fine one day then all of a sudden, the heavens would turn black, the rain would absolutely piss down with thunder and lightning. It really affected everything that you did; vehicles became bogged down

on the few roads that were available. This was not only a pain in the arse as we had to get them out, but they caused roadblocks for hours, sometimes a couple of days. You got filthy dirty and you were wet through most of the time. The damp affected your clothing which would rot in no time, you had the constant problem of keeping your weapons and ammunition in a ready state of function and then there was for many of us the problem of keeping your cigarettes dry. There always seemed to be millions more biting insects in the air during the wet season too – this was day and night and a constant torment to all of us. Just one day in those jungles felt like an eternity of hardship and pain. It was an incredibly demanding environment that you could say you never really got used to.

Generally, there are three types of jungle: primary, secondary and coastal. Primary jungle consists of natural vegetation which has never been interfered with by man or machine and has remained unchanged over the centuries. In primary jungles visibility is often limited to less than thirty yards, depending on the slope of the terrain and amount of vegetation present. Streams in primary jungle can become blocked, forming swampy areas which in turn often become impassable. Of course, swamp areas can always be circumvented but good navigation is required to then regain the original line of travel. The term 'impassable' is of course misleading, as no jungle is impassable: new routes around swamp and foliage can be cut with the aid of a machete which most troops were issued with.

Secondary jungle is often the product of local cultivation where sections of jungle have been cleared of vegetation which is then permitted to regrow. Usually secondary jungle is comprised of very thick ferns, brambles and grasses. Often the only way of tackling such terrain is to walk over it as opposed to trying to cut through it. Tommie Watkins recalled this type of jungle terrain:

With an absence of tall trees, there was little in the way of shade; the heat of the sun were unbearable at the best of times, but in trying to negotiate your way through thick bushes, thorns and grass it was very easy to succumb to the heat which was quite hot, I can tell you. It was kind of like being shut in a very hot steamy room, there was no air and there was no shade. This coupled with your own exertions exacerbated the problems and it could become difficult to breathe. The thorns on some of the bushes were lethal; they'd tear your clothing to shreds and any uncovered skin could be cut to ribbons too. When we talk of grass in the jungles of Asia, it's not like the grass we have here in England. It was tall enough to conceal an elephant, and some varieties had razor-sharp edges. It was just thoroughly unpleasant in every aspect and demanded maximum effort of every man passing through it.

Coastal jungle tends to be more open, consisting of grass that can grow to a height of eight feet, and of course there are the mangrove swamps. The close proximity of both to the ocean, however, does not mean coastal areas are any cooler; in fact, quite the contrary. Coastal jungle as with secondary retains heat due to the tall grass and the lack of tree cover. Visibility is also as much an issue as that experienced with both primary and secondary jungle terrain.

The heat and high humidity experienced in the jungle means that if one is to operate within it effectively, then sufficient hydration becomes a critical factor, along with avoiding heatstroke where possible. One British Fourteenth Army sergeant described the heat in the jungles of Burma:

It was a suffocating, humid heat; if you could imagine being shut inside a hot greenhouse on the hottest day of the year and the heating being turned on inside it, and times it by five or ten, then you'd experience something of what it was like. The heat not only physically drains you; it requires you to take on board more fluids than you would do so normally. Regular slugs of water rather than drinking down a whole canteen full was the best method of staying hydrated. You wore a hat to keep the sun off your head if you were anywhere that was exposed to sunlight. These are just the first problems you must deal with though. The heat and humidity can cause even the smallest scratch to become infected within hours. I recall one fellow was negotiating a slope among some trees and he was rather foolishly using his government-issue machete as a kind of walking stick to help him get down the bank. He slipped and as he lost his grip on the machete, his hand slid down the blade. It sliced his hand open badly and I knew then this man had a serious injury that anywhere else could be dealt with easily. The wound became infected in a short time; it turned yellow, purple and green pus began to ooze from it. If it were not for the local Indians who knew how to deal with these things, that man might have lost his hand to gangrene. It was an elderly Indian woman who used some local herbal plant formula to treat the infected wound. Her remedy was not without its own pains, as she burned a tarlike substance made from leaves or plants into the wound, but it worked and the man did recover, though he would have had a nasty scar for a souvenir.

Terrain itself could prove a danger as hills, rocky crags and steep slopes all had to be negotiated. There were many falls resulting in broken arms, legs or other more severe injuries including death. If a man became injured due to a fall, it was a serious setback as a wounded man tied up resources and treatment was not always nearby. Tommie Watkins recalled:

We once had to cross the top of a waterfall. The water was not deep, only just below the knees but the force it moved at was quite surprising. There were lots of rocks, so we used these to negotiate our way across the water. The drop from the waterfall was around twenty-five feet and the water fell into a pool below. The water was probably deep enough for you to dive into, but it was studded with sharp-looking rocks sticking up out of the pool. If one of us had gone over the falls due to a slip or whatever, then a serious injury or death was a certainty. There was some terrain in the jungle that had deep crevices that if a man fell in, there would be no means of extricating him even if he were still alive. Some of these crevices were hundreds of feet deep.

We learned this from the tribespeople. Just the thought of that made you think very carefully when out on patrol or moving out. The terrain was a bloody nightmare in the best of conditions; in the monsoon it was a hundred times worse.

Due to the high humidity in the jungle there were many trees that had rotted through. These presented the obvious dangers of falling trees, a frequent occurrence in some areas, both day and night. One soldier wrote:

> Tree falls were quite regular in our sector. You'd hear a loud cracking noise then a tree would come crashing down, sometimes far away, sometimes very close. In the dark you couldn't gauge whether the tree was going to hit or miss you. You would instinctively curl up into a foetal position and pray. Your rest was often interrupted by this near-constant plague. Yet in other areas there were hardly any tree falls. Danger from the jungle came in so many forms.

Foot rot was another common problem. It was not often a soldier had the luxury of dry socks and boots, due to the conditions. Special foot powders were issued but even these could not always prevent the onset of what is often termed as 'trench foot', an age-old affliction suffered by soldiers on military campaigns. It is caused primarily by the feet being constantly exposed to wet, or wet and cold, conditions. Jungle-issue boots were often designed to dry out quickly with the aid of a campfire, but the combination of heat and humidity meant that a soldier often walked around in wet or damp boots for days, even weeks, particularly in the monsoon season. Trench foot came in varying degrees of severity. In jungle climates the feet often became infected with swollen sores or fungal infections that spread to the toes. One such case of jungle foot rot comes from an army medic's account described below:

> The man in question had been getting steadily worse; he began to limp, and his walking was then reduced to hobbling. When his boots were removed, the smell was quite beyond description. The skin was wrinkled, pockmarked with sores; the skin between the toes had begun to almost decompose and the toenails were yellow and thickened. When a man's

feet end up like this, it renders him inoperable as he cannot move quickly enough. The only recommendations we as medics can offer is (a) removing wet footwear at night including socks, to aid in the drying of boots and to keep the feet reasonably aired, (b) the use of anti-fungal foot powders as issued in theatre, (c) replace wet socks with dry ones wherever possible. Trench Foot has been the plague of the soldier for centuries; in dry conditions it soon clears with treatment but here in this hot damp climate where soldiers are constantly having to cross streams and rivers it is a problem.

The natural hazards in these environments are many and varied. In the jungles of Asia there are many species of snake that are potentially dangerous to humans, including Indian cobras, common kraits, Russell's viper, and carpet vipers. Though there are many other varieties of snake which can also be considered as dangerous in this part of the world, one such example being the Burmese python. This is one of the five largest species of snakes in the world and is widespread throughout southern and South-East Asia. These large snakes are nocturnal hunters by nature and are as at home in rivers and swamps as they are in trees. As they grow and their weight and size increases, they tend to restrict their movements to the ground, where they can be encountered by the unwary. While these large snakes are capable of killing and consuming large prey such as deer, wild pigs, crocodiles, jungle cats and unwary primates, they are not thought to actively seek out human beings as prey items, yet they have been known to kill and consume humans. Ron Rastal, a former British soldier with the Fourteenth Army, recalled:

> Snakes were one of my biggest fears. We'd heard about the different types of snakes we could easily encounter in the jungles of Asia; I wasn't keen on meeting any of them in particular [he laughs]. I do recall one incident with a snake which was hanging from a tree directly in the path of our patrol. The lead man just stopped and pointed at the snake. None of us wanted to duck down and walk under it, and we were just about to go around it when one of the Gurkha soldiers with us just marches up to this snake, grabs hold

of the head and with one swift chop removes the head of the reptile with his kukri knife. We thought, 'You mad little fucker' and did we laugh about that later. The snake had a body as thick as a car's tyre; it was of a type that crushes or constricts its prey. The Gurkhas used to tell us these animals are not usually aggressive, but a smart man will avoid them if he can. We had to be aware of cobras and kraits which infested certain areas of the jungle. If we encountered any of these, the idea was to back away very slowly, give the creature room and move away from it. If any of these were to bite you then your chances of seeing home again were slim, especially if out in the jungle where specialist treatment could be hours or even days away. No, I didn't like snakes anyway; I fucking hated the things. I'd only ever seen them in zoos previously, and I can remember sitting down and thinking, 'Here I am and there could be a snake right beside me or up in the tree I'm sitting under.' Yes, I became more than a little paranoid you could say [he laughs].

Snakebite kits were issued to Allied forces operating in jungle environments, usually supplied to the medics, field hospital staff and sometimes as a piece of personal kit to the soldiers themselves. These Second World War snakebite kits when compared to the anti-venom countermeasures of today were somewhat primitive. For example, one such kit gave the following instructions for use in the case of a snake bite.

1. Apply tourniquet at once, placing it between body and bite. Apply above knee in foot and leg bites. Loosen tourniquet every 20 minutes for 10–15 seconds.
2. Apply iodine to the area around the bite.
3. Paint lancet blade with iodine.
4. Make cross incision quarter of an inch long and quarter of an inch deep over each fang mark.
5. Use oval cup for finger and toes; for flatter surfaces use round cup which fits best over place where incisions have been made.
6. Place cup tightly over incisions, and apply suction by pressing and then releasing plunger. Suction can be increased by repeating this movement.

7. Continue suction for 20 minutes before loosening tourniquet. Repeat suction for at least three 20-minute periods.
8. In case of faintness, crush ammonia inhalant container and hold near nose.
9. If breathing becomes difficult or shows signs of stopping, give artificial respiration by prone pressure method.
10. If there is great bleeding from the incisions, tighten tourniquets further. If this does not stop the rapid bleeding, press finger firmly over incisions.
11. After suction has been completed sprinkle sulfanilamide into incisions and apply a sterile dressing.

Some snakebite instructions also advised the sucking of venom from a bite wound, which we now know to be totally ineffective, as a snake's fangs penetrate like hypodermic needles, the venom being injected too deep to be removed orally. Considering the number of venomous snakes prevalent in Asia and their close proximity to the troops, there were only two recorded cases of British soldiers being killed by snakebite in the Second World War. However, soldiers of other nations involved in the jungle war at the time may have differing statistics on the issue. Snakes were undoubtedly an issue worthy of the highest consideration, yet the fear they instilled was out of proportion to the actual threat they posed.

Spiders, although often wrongly portrayed as the creatures of many a nightmare, were also a common sight in the jungle environment. The Yellow Sac spider (Cheiracanthium punctorium) prevalent throughout Central Asia has fangs capable of penetrating human skin. While the bite of this relatively small (15mm) spider is not thought to pose any significant threat, some adverse reactions which include sharp pain that can last up to ten days, nausea and vomiting and necrosis of the tissues surrounding the bite area have been recorded by those unfortunate enough to have been bitten.

Some of the most feared – and for good reason – spiders in the jungles of Asia are undoubtedly the arboreal (tree-dwelling) tarantulas such as the Indian ornamental tarantula (Poecilotheria regalis). These spiders generally have a leg span of six to eight inches and potent venom. Although no recorded deaths due to a tarantula bite have yet been recorded in the jungles of Asia, they were greatly feared by both

British and Japanese soldiers. Encounters with these spiders leading to bites were often purely accidental, as Ron Rastal recalls:

> You could just be going through bushes and one of these things could drop on you as you disturbed the tree branches. The greatest fear of many a man was having one of these drop on you as you cut your way through the bush. They had a chalky-white- and black-patterned body with vivid blue and yellow colours on their undersides. They moved as fast as lightning and would often flee from any disturbance, but one fellow had one fall into his shirt. Of course, he began flapping around like a lunatic and that's when the spider bit him on the lower abdomen. The bite as he described it was one of the worst pains he had ever felt in his life. He said it felt like someone had poured petrol on that part of his body and had lit it. He was in agony for a few days and totally useless until the effects of the venom wore off. You had to beware while cutting through bushes and trees and if you saw evidence of webs, then you had to be very careful to not go in there like a bull in a china shop as they used to say.

Apart from spiders, other members of the arachnid family call the jungle home, the most notorious being that of the scorpion. The Asian forest scorpion, although intimidating in appearance, was considered relatively harmless. Its sting was said to be much the same as that of a bee. Either way an unwelcome visitor if discovered in a boot or kitbag as was often the case. Ron Rastal recalls:

> It was nice to be able to take your boots off even if just for a while. It wasn't always permitted in case of ambush or other emergency. You didn't want to be fumbling around putting boots on if suddenly attacked at night or daytime; it was impractical for obvious reasons. If you did take your boots off it was always advisable to hang them from a tree branch or something and within reach. The scorpions we saw were large black-bodied things; they looked more threatening than they actually were. Some of the Indian and Gurkha soldiers thought it was great fun to grab these

things by their tails and bring them to show you. I knew of men getting stung on the foot because one had got inside a boot, but the stings were not that bad and did not contain the venom that some of the spiders and centipedes had. Even so, I didn't like anything that either crawled or flew and stung.

Another of the soldiers' most loathed jungle companions was that of the giant jungle centipede. These creatures posed a significant threat as their bite was not only said to have been an 'excruciation beyond description', but their venom was one of the most potent of the insect world. The Asian jungles were infested with these large aggressive centipedes which would often bite without provocation. It was always wise after a night in the jungle to check boots if left off, kitbags and any clothing which had been removed the night before. Bites from these giant centipedes were not only capable of rendering a soldier useless for an extended period of time due to the severity of pain experienced but the wound itself could become so badly suppurated due to the necrotizing effect of the venom that in some cases a limb would have to be amputated. Amputation cases were rare, but the threat certainly did exist with these creatures, and they demanded absolute respect. Tommie Watkins recalled:

Those centipedes were bloody big things; they used to give me the creeps. Some areas were infested with the things and we knew they could catch and kill rats, mice, large spiders and other things too. They had these large curved fangs either side of their heads, which is what they used to bite you with. If one latched onto you, it would wrap itself around your arm or hand and bite you multiple times. I heard of men becoming really sick after being bitten. You'd lie awake at night wondering if that itch you felt was one crawling up your leg. It was certainly something that threatened the morale of men in the jungle. The Japs must have had much the same problems as what we did; I guessed they must have hated these things as much as we did.

Ants, prevalent in Asian jungles, were not so much a threat, but more a nuisance factor for those engaged in jungle combat. Before any camp could be set up, the area firstly had to be checked for the presence of ant nests. It was never considered wise to set up camp near ant nests or colonies. The giant forest ant (D.gigas) was a familiar and fascinating sight to all those engaged in warfare in the jungles of Asia. These ants, while very large, are generally not an aggressive species yet can deliver a painful bite and setting up camp too near a nest of these ants was not the best idea for obvious reasons.

Those entering the jungles of Asia were also warned to beware of jungle cats such as panthers and tigers. Although generally shy animals that will in many cases attempt to avoid confrontation with humans, they did – and still do – pose a threat to life in some cases. Tigers in particular were (and are) notorious for raiding jungle villages and carrying off unwary victims; often where pickings were good, the animal would keep returning until it was either shot or trapped. There are many well documented cases of tigers becoming maneaters and Tommie Watkins recalls:

> We were warned to beware of tigers. I was told about a village in India where the Indians had buried some bodies and one tiger was attracted to the scent of the decaying meat, I suppose. The animal would exhume the bodies and drag them off somewhere safe to feed on them. The locals believed it was some jungle demon [he laughs], being the superstitious souls they were. It was only when a villager was ambushed and dragged off in broad daylight in front of other villagers by a large male tiger that they understood what it was. By providing food in the form of buried corpses, they were unwittingly attracting an animal that had developed a taste for human flesh and would keep returning. In the end, after it had raided the village several more times killing two and injuring a young boy, a group of men set out to kill the animal. They tracked it for four days but returned to the village with the tiger's body as a trophy.
>
> So yes, we understood the dangers, that you didn't go off on your own into the jungle, and to be wary around sources of water where these animals often ambushed their prey. In all my time in Asia I only had one fleeting glimpse of a tiger as it ran across a rice paddy and into the jungle the other end.

As for panthers I never saw any of those. Apparently, they are timid creatures which flee upon hearing you approach; you can walk right past one and not even see or hear it. They have the power to bring down a fully grown silverback gorilla, so I was told, so they deserve respect.

From my own experiences I would say that wild pigs, elephants, buffalos and crocodiles posed more of a danger to us than any jungle cats. Wild pig would charge without hesitation if startled and could inflict very nasty injuries. Buffalos were the same, bloody evil-tempered things that would charge you without provocation, especially in mating season or if they had young. Elephants we tried to avoid and give plenty of room, but it wasn't always easy in combat situations. I know elephants were shot on more than one occasion after charging a patrol. Crocodiles were another really huge concern. They infested swamps and rivers and we heard the Japs were having just as many problems with them as what we were. Crossing swamps and rivers required careful navigation and extreme vigilance. If you had to cross a river or any water, you tried to cross at the shallowest point with the least distance to the other side. It wasn't always that easy though; nothing was in the jungle. Most jungle operations required stealth – you couldn't go around blasting everything that moved with your .303 Enfield, otherwise your enemy would have been alerted to your presence. Sometimes you just had to deal with things as hard as they may have seemed. Yes, you just had to deal with it; that's how it was.

Leeches were another misery common to soldiers fighting in the jungle. Leeches can be as long as three to five centimetres when outstretched. They latch on to either a human or animal, with their jaws injecting an anti-coagulant called hirudin, which acts to prevent the host's blood from clotting, thus enabling a continuous flow of blood for the leech to feed on. Generally, the larger the leech the greater the amount of hirudin injected. Hirudin is such a powerful anti-coagulant that a leech bite can continue bleeding for several hours after the leech has dropped off after having had its fill of blood. The good news is that leeches neither carry nor transmit any harmful diseases. This, of course, was no endearing factor to the soldiers who sometimes found leeches a constant companion. When I asked Tommie Watkins about his experiences of leeches, he recalled:

> Bloody things – excuse the pun there. We all had leeches on us at some point, and we detested them. You couldn't pull them off; if you did there was a chance the jaws of the creature would remain in your skin which could become infected as most wounds do in jungle conditions. No, we often burned them off with a cigarette. If you didn't smoke, you'd ask a mate who did to save you the butt of his fag so you could burn any leeches off you with it. Stick a fag end on one and they'd drop off in an instant. If there were no fag ends available, you could always stick a pin in them; they didn't like that either [he laughs]. A lot of lads hated crossing rivers or streams because of leeches. They were worried about leeches getting on their cocks or bollocks. We can laugh about it now, but we didn't back then I can tell you.

Of all the creatures that reside in the jungle it is perhaps no surprise then that the smallest of all posed the greatest threat to a soldier's physical well-being. This baleful honour goes to the mosquito.

Mosquitos were and still are a constant nuisance in tropical regions where they thrive in their millions. Bites from mosquitos carrying certain viruses or parasites can cause severe illness. Infected mosquitos can transmit infections such as yellow fever, malaria, West Nile virus, dengue fever along with some forms of brain infection commonly known as encephalitis in the clinical profession. It is the female mosquito which possesses a mouthpart capable of piercing skin to siphon off blood from its host. The mosquito obtains a virus or parasite by biting an infected person or animal, which is then transferred when biting you. The male mosquito lacks this blood-sucking ability as it does not produce eggs and so has no need for the proteins found in the blood of humans or animals. Nonetheless, they are equally as irritating, as any person who has encountered them will testify.

Akihara Koto recalls:

> Mosquitos infested the jungles of Asia; there must have been millions of them there. Wherever we marched,

fought or rested, the clouds of biting mosquitos were ever present. At night if you did not sleep with a net over yourself it would be impossible to sleep at all as the bites were so irritating. I know of men who were driven almost insane by biting mosquitos, so your mosquito net was as essential a piece of equipment as your rifle. Mosquitos made life hard, but they also made life hard for our enemy too, so it was not just us suffering from them.

Around the world there were and still are what are termed indigenous people who call the jungle home. Many of these peoples comprise distinct, vulnerable tribes that possess only a limited ability to participate in, and are most often marginalized by, the development process of the urbanized societies which live around them. Many do not appreciate intrusion into what is after all their home territory. There was initially much myth surrounding the tribes of Indians who inhabited the jungles of Asia and Burma. There is no doubt that some of these tribes reacted aggressively, and with their primitive weaponry did attempt some form of resistance, yet the firepower at the disposal of both Allied and Japanese forces in comparison to these tribes was astronomical. Any aggression if encountered was often met with a swift and deadly response. The Allied forces were far more diplomatic and sympathetic towards any indigenous people they encountered during their jungle excursions. They understood that these tribes could prove a useful ally in the war against the Japanese, while the Japanese often simply raped and murdered, destroying homes and plundering any livestock and crops in the process. Many indigenous tribes learned to despise the Japanese as much as their western enemies yet bringing them on side was no easy process due not only to the obvious language barriers but cultural ones too. Tommie Watkins recalls:

> I think most of us expected it to be like the old black and white Tarzan films we had watched as kids at the picture shows [he laughs]; you know, jungle drums, cannibals and head-hunters and things like that. The things the Japanese had done to these people was disgusting and our aim was to treat them with respect and maybe they would take our side in a war which they had no choice in. Their value as

trackers and their natural instinct of being able to read the jungle from the sounds of its animals and things would prove invaluable to us against the Japs who just killed these people if they encountered them. The tribes believed the war going on around them was nothing to do with them: they hadn't started it and their logic was that they just wanted to live in peace and for people to leave them alone. I know some just went deeper into the jungle in the hope that the war would be left behind. I heard some random stories of blowpipes with poison darts being shot at our soldiers or the odd arrow being fired, the odd spear being thrown. How true were these stories I have no idea.

While by no means exhaustive, this chapter serves as a sobering reflection of what is the law of the jungle and the unique challenges faced by the soldiers who had to eat, sleep and fight within its sometimes dark, claustrophobic confines.

Chapter 4

Above the Jungle Canopy

As the Japanese army and naval air forces had such influence upon the successes of its forces on the ground, it is worthy of some examination here.

The first aerial engagements between the air forces of the Japanese Empire and those of the British Commonwealth, primarily throughout the Malaya–Singapore campaign of 1941/2, proved a disaster, particularly for the Royal Air Force. Throughout this period the Japanese air force dominated the skies, inflicting a humiliating and decisive defeat upon the RAF. The reasons behind Japan's dominance of the skies over Malaya and Singapore is easily explained. Japanese staff officers had conducted a thorough analysis of their future enemies' capabilities, equipment and tactics, particularly by studying facets of the air war which took place over Europe and the Mediterranean theatres of 1939–41. It was the theoretical groundwork that would provide the foundations for the early Japanese successes. In comparison the British government, along with its military commanders, had been wholly ignorant in their knowledge of Japanese aircraft, weaponry, tactics and units. To say that the capabilities of the Japanese air force had been underestimated would be an understatement.

To the contrary, the Japanese had produced some of the finest fighter aircraft of the day, particularly in the Mitsubishi A6M Zero (designed by Jiro Horikoshi) and the Nakajima Ki-43 'Oscar' (designed by Hideo Itokawa). The Mitsubishi A6M Zero was without doubt one of the finest fighter aircraft of the Second World War, manufactured by the Mitsubishi Aircraft Company, a part of Mitsubishi Heavy Industries. The Zero served as a carrier-borne fighter with the Japanese Imperial Navy from 1940 to the war's end in 1945. It was referred to as the Zero by its pilots due to '0' being the last digit of the imperial year 2600 (1940), the year the aircraft entered service with the Imperial Navy.

The Zero was an exemplary aircraft to fly, combining excellent manoeuvrability, range and firepower with the respectable maximum speed of 346mph. Its armament of two 7.7mm Type 97 machine guns (with 500 rounds per gun) mounted above the engine and fixed to fire forward through the propeller and a 20mm Type 99-1 cannon (with 60 rounds per gun) in each wing was a formidable armament for its day, and more than adequate to knock any Allied fighter then in service out of the sky. Although primarily a carrier-based navy fighter, the A6M2 Zero was also frequently used as a land-based fighter aircraft. The Zero soon proved itself an excellent dogfighting aircraft, achieving an outstanding kill ratio of 12 to 1. It would remain the nemesis of the British, Commonwealth and American air forces until mid-1942 when a steady influx of new, superior Allied aircraft in combination with the introduction of new tactics meant that the Allied pilots were at least able to engage the Zeros on a generally equal basis. The major drawbacks of the Zero were its lack of armour protection for its pilot, an inability to fit newer and more powerful engines and lack of hydraulic flaps and rudder that had an adverse effect on performance at high speeds. Much like an ageing boxer refusing retirement, the Zero steadily declined in its effectiveness and by 1944 was considered outdated in comparison to the newer Allied fighter aircraft then entering service. It is unfitting that the Zero, the once all-conquering aerial weapon, would end its days in the kamikaze role, an undignified end for such a supreme aircraft.

The Nakajima Ki-43 Hayabusa (peregrine falcon) had been conceived as a single-engined, land-based tactical fighter aircraft specifically for use by the Imperial Japanese Army Air Force. The brainchild of Japanese aircraft designer Hideo Itokawa, the Ki-43 was constructed by the Nakajima Aircraft Company and entered service in October 1941. The Allies referred to the Ki-43 as 'Oscar' but was also often known as the 'Army Zero' due to its similarity in design to the Mitsubishi A6M Zero. It is true that both the Ki-43 and A6M Zero were born of a similar layout, utilizing the same Nakajima Sakae radial engine with its characteristic rounded cowlings, and with bubble-type cockpit canopies. The Ki-43 was slightly slower than the A6M Zero with a top speed of 333mph. Often in the heat of air-to-air combat the Ki-43 was mistakenly reported as being a Zero on numerous occasions by Allied pilots. This was puzzling for Allied air intelligence departments who were led to believe that Zeros had been encountered in areas of operation where there were no navy fighters present. As with the A6M Zero, the Ki-43 proved a formidable adversary during the early phase of the war despite its lack of armour protection – the Achilles heel of many Japanese aircraft – and absence of vital self-sealing fuel tanks. The Ki-43 was highly manoeuvrable, light weight and very easy to fly, yet unlike the A6M Zero its armament was considered too light. The Ki-43 was armed with just a pair of 12.7mm (.50 calibre) H0-103 heavy machine guns for the air-to-air combat role. These two machine guns were fitted above the engine and fixed to fire forward through the propeller blade, the two guns being belt-fed a capacity of 270 rounds per gun. Even by early Second World War standards, this two-machine gun armament was considered insufficient for aerial combat, yet despite its lightweight punch the Ki-43 proved a success. Despite being an extremely difficult aircraft to hit in a dogfight, it did have a tendency to catch fire easily and even break up in the air upon receiving hits. Despite these factors the Nakajima Ki-43 shot down more Allied aircraft than any other Japanese fighter. Almost all of the Japanese Army Air Force 'aces' claimed their kills while flying the Ki-43. As with the A6M Zero, as the sun began to set on Japanese military supremacy, the Ki-43 was allocated to the kamikaze role against the US Navy.

What was it like for a Japanese fighter pilot during the early years of glory over the jungles of Asia? How did they live and what did they think about their experiences in relation to those troops they were supporting on the ground? When I began my research into this area of the Japanese military, I was fearful of coming up against a brick wall, with few options other than to consult existing volumes available on the subject at the time. It was an elderly researcher who lived in the same village as I did at the time who gave me a few leads, including the address of the then Zero Fighters' Association in Japan. Back in those days there were still many former Japanese Zero fighter pilots around (unlike today), and they were surprisingly willing to talk about their service, despite there still being much animosity towards the Japanese at the time. Just like Nazi Germany it was not fashionable back then to try and interview 'the enemy' and such endeavours had to be kept secret from those British veterans I was talking with at the time for fear of them 'clamming up' and refusing to talk to me any further. Feelings were still very evidently hostile despite the passing of many years since 1945 and I learned to tread very carefully, as I knew success depended on being considerate to all of those who were then contributing to the work that would result in this book.

With the commencement of hostilities, the Allied forces in Malaya and Singapore had at their disposal four fighter squadrons: 21 and 453 RAAF (Royal Australian Air Force), 243 RAF (Royal Air Force) and 488 RNAF (Royal New Zealand Air Force). These four fighter squadrons were equipped with the Brewster Buffalo B-399E, fighter an aircraft described by many as dangerously inadequate in terms of performance and armament. It was often referred to as a 'barrel with wings' by many of the pilots who flew it and many Buffalo pilots had a universal dislike of the aircraft, which they felt put them at an instant disadvantage against the Japanese. It was an aircraft characterized by its engine's fuel starvation problems, poor supercharger performance at higher altitudes, and a tendency to overheat in the tropical climate. The technical issues combined with its poor armament (four .50-calibre machine guns), inadequate maximum speed and near non-existent manoeuvrability meant that no matter how good the pilot was at its controls, it was a sitting duck in many aspects of the air campaign over Malaya and Singapore against superior Japanese opposition. What were the thoughts of the Allied pilots given the seemingly insurmountable task of taking on the Ki-43 and Zero in combat knowing they were at such an overwhelming aerial disadvantage? Former Flying Officer Michael Read Wright recalled the situation at the time:

> The thought of flying against the Ki-43 was a bad enough proposition. We understood the limitations of our aeroplanes only too well; we knew in a sense we had no way of competing with the Japanese pilots on an even level. Both the Ki-43 and the Zero were faster, and of course more manoeuvrable than our lumbering Buffalo fighters. We encountered mainly Ki-43 fighters which we knew were fast, very agile yet only carried two machine guns to our four. The problem was if your aircraft's performance was below par then you stood little chance of getting on the enemy's tail to use your four machine guns on him. The Zero was something we came to dread as it was armed with two 20mm cannons. Going up against Zeros was suicide, no matter how good you were as a pilot; if your aeroplane was poor your chances of survival

were slim indeed. In combat against the Ki-43 and Zero survival depended purely on your experience. Being an older pre-Second World War pilot, I had more experience than many of the younger men on our squadrons, yet with inferior speed and overall performance, even my experience counted for very little.

I was once in the process of taking off when I was attacked from above and astern. The Japanese plane put bullets into my engine; I saw the strikes of his machine-gun rounds and I just thought, 'Shit, now you're in big fucking trouble.' At that same instant steam quickly followed by oil coated my windscreen and all I could do was shut off the engine as I had not gathered sufficient speed at that point; thankfully for me, I was able to stop the aircraft before hitting a bank of trees at the end of the runway. I jumped out of the aircraft and ran into the trees for cover. The Japs made several passes, firstly firing into my aircraft which soon caught fire as it was full of fuel, then they made passes firing into other aircraft and then into the trees where I had run. They were obviously gunning for me, but I was quite safe where I was apart from the fact I had ran and jumped into an ants' nest. Jungle ants don't take kindly to someone diving onto their nests and I received some very painful stings for my trouble. These were my only wounds; I was very lucky as others had fared less fortunately than myself. Had I made it into the air, I very much doubt I could have made any difference and may have ended up dead for my trouble. After this debacle, it was just chaos and fear everywhere; it was clear we could not at that moment compete with the Japanese fighters. What we needed were P-40s, Hurricanes or Spitfires – not bloody Brewster Buffalos. We hated everything about them, and I agree with most historians' hypotheses that these aircraft were death traps.

In the eyes of the average Japanese fighter pilot who had gained valuable experience in air-to-air combat over China and Russia, the Buffalo was viewed as a comical opponent. Hikokuru Ishimaru who flew the Zero recalled:

We knew from our intelligence reports that the enemy squadrons tasked with defending Malaya and Singapore were equipped with very inferior fighter aircraft, that they were short on spare parts and were in effect poorly organized. Therefore, our confidence was very high and whenever we took off on a combat mission to attack enemy airfields, we were excited to get into battle. The battles themselves were not exactly battles of any honour; we often surprised them on the ground and used our machine guns to destroy them. With just a few seconds of fire, the Buffalos blew up, and any which did get airborne were easy targets as they could not compete with our superior machines. I felt honoured to fly a Zero: it was an exceptional fighting aeroplane.

The Buffalo was easy prey for us; I shot two of them down during my service until we were relocated. My method was to use my superior speed as the Buffalo could not outmanoeuvre me; it was a case of getting on his tail and often having to reduce power. I would look behind to ensure an enemy was not sneaking up on me, then I would fire my two 20mm cannons and two machine guns for two seconds. It was a leisurely action on my part. I would watch as my cannon shells exploded and tore him to pieces, pieces would fall away and, as I dived away to observe, I would watch him spiral down and then crash into the ground below. I was elated as it was a victory not only for me personally but my country too. Had the enemy sent better aircraft, our skills may have been tested more appropriately.

Of course, this soon began to happen, and we faced a better enemy as the fighting progressed, yet even then I did not ever feel intimidated by my enemy or at any disadvantage to him. Our main aim overall was to destroy the enemy fighters and any bomber aircraft they had on the ground. Ground attack operations were very simple, though you had to be aware of possible anti-aircraft fire. The anti-aircraft guns fired 2lb high-explosive shells at high rates of fire and were more a danger to us than their fighters during the early phase of the war. We would often task some of our aircraft to bomb or strafe these anti-aircraft guns, leaving us to concentrate on any aircraft on the ground or any that had got into the air.

Flying Officer Wright adds further analysis to Hikokuru Ishimaru's summary of the situation of the air war at the time:

Perhaps one of the greatest problems we faced in the Malaya/Singapore defence in the air war was the lack of any early warning. The airfields we had were difficult enough to defend as it was, but without any real detection apparatus to let us know in advance that an enemy air attack was inbound, we were totally blind. Therefore, in general, we got hammered on the ground and most of our aircraft were lost either on the ground or as they attempted to take off to intercept the Japanese. Once they were over the airfield the odds of you being able to get into the air and challenge them were very slim indeed. It does not do your morale any good when you see one of your friends trying to get airborne and then seconds later you see him bursting into flames and cartwheeling into the jungle; you would see that he was burning to death and you knew it could very likely be you the next time. It was incredibly frustrating and if we had the right aircraft and effective early warning, I think we could have done better than just taking pot shots and withdrawing all the time, which of course is what we did.

Do I see it as a humiliation? Yes, it was humiliating in some respects as we were assured the Japanese air force were limited in capability, that their pilots were not as well trained as what we were, and their aircraft were limited to old obsolete types. Yes, it all came as a shock, didn't it, and quite to the contrary the Japanese were very well trained, well organized and equipped with some excellent fighter and bomber aircraft. We in effect didn't stand a chance at that point. I recall before we had to withdraw from our first airfield feeling very angry indeed. We had been sent here to defend Malaya and Singapore with aircraft that were not fit for purpose; when anything went wrong with them, we could not get any spares. We were annoyed by the conditions we had to live in and the adverse weather conditions, mosquitos and other biting insects; the food was pretty terrible and everything got damp including your treasured letters from home. It was hell; no other word can describe it accurately. We felt as if we were on the back foot, constantly having to relocate, set up tents and quarters all over again and all the time being jumped by Japanese aircraft.

I was lucky enough to shoot down a couple of Nakajima Ki-27 fighters during the first withdrawal, but the Japanese just sent more of their Ki-43s. There were some tales of immense heroism against these overwhelming odds. A little known one is the selfless courage and bravery displayed by that of Sergeant Malcolm Neville Read of 453 Squadron, Royal Australian Air Force. This brave and courageous Aussie sacrificed himself in air-to-air combat by ramming his Brewster Buffalo fighter into a Nakajima Ki-43 of the 64th Sentai over Kuala Lumpur on 22 December 1941. Both Sergeant Read and his Japanese opponent were killed in this incident. Sergeant Read could have turned and fled but this action was typical of the Australians' sheer bravery and aggression against the Japanese. The Aussies hated them with a passion; they were very good pilots and displayed great courage throughout the whole of the war.

The Japanese relished the superiority they were enjoying over their western enemies, as Hikokuru Ishimaru gleefully recounted:

We felt happy at our progress and after we returned from our operations we would celebrate in the traditional Japanese manner. We would have a meal of rice and seafood and we would drink sake and talk of our tactics and how we did in the battle. We understood that at some point the odds could change, that better enemy aircraft could come but we felt no fear and felt it more a challenge than anything, a challenge which we would face as warriors when the time came. Our airfields were not that different to our white enemies;

we lived in the same climate, in tents and hastily erected camps. We had to contend with all the same things such as mosquitos and other unpleasant creatures, yet we were better prepared from a psychological point, I think, and we had the better fighter aircraft at that time to do the job.

When we did well, we pilots were rewarded: young women were brought to us from the nearby villages and we were happy to receive their services. Some of the pilots were young married men and declined the offers of the girls, but we who did not have a wife back home were like as they say children in a candy shop. I sometimes had two or three of them in one night.

It was a time of much glory and much confidence for us. The idea was to maintain the pressure on the enemy and keep forcing them back. We were winning the war against them and yes, things were good at that point. The one day it rained incessantly and we could not fly, so we went sightseeing. We went to have a look at a couple of enemy planes that had been shot down; one was a Buffalo, the other a Hudson twin-engined aircraft. The Buffalo was partially buried in the ground, the wings had torn off and we could only find one. There was no pilot in the seat of the Buffalo, yet the seat was covered in dry blood and there were a lot of blood splashes in the cockpit. A local pointed out a grave which had been dug where the pilot had been interred. I took out my knife and prised out one of the dials from the Buffalo's control panel as a trophy. I still have it now, somewhere. There were a few rounds of live ammunition scattered around the site. We picked them up and examined them before throwing them into the jungle. The Hudson was completely smashed into the ground with wreckage over a wide area. We looked around it and examined one of the propeller blades that had sheared off in the impact. One of the pilots with us decided he wanted to take it back to the airfield with him as a personal trophy. It was amusing as he dragged it for some yards before it grew too cumbersome and he dropped it. As we were all friends, we helped carry it back for him. He said he wanted to send it home to his family in Japan and I think he managed to do it. It was amusing some of the things that happened.

I recall one evening one of the pilots in our hut (which was made from wood and jungle foliage) waking up and running around like a demon, shouting and flailing his arms like a bird trying to take off. We woke and wondered what was going on, and he pointed to where he had been sleeping. As one man held a lamp over his bed, I could see a giant jungle centipede crawling around over it. I grabbed a machete and slashed at the creature, cutting it in half. These giant centipedes could be very dangerous indeed; their bites were said to be painful and venomous. This was one of the problems with jungle habitation – spiders and centipedes or snakes trying to share your sleeping quarters with you. I wasn't afraid of snakes, but spiders, centipedes and scorpions were things I was afraid of as some were considered deadly to humans. Frequently a man would leap out of his bed in the night when a snake slithered in beside him; it was funny for us but not him. The best method was to just lie perfectly still until the reptile passed and slithered away.

Japanese dominance of the air continued forcing Allied air assets back to Singapore. 64 Squadron had fared dreadfully, running out of aircraft to the point where its surviving ground crews were shipped out to Burma. 1 and 8 RAAF squadrons were amalgamated due to the severity of aircraft losses. This had a detrimental effect upon Allied ground forces and shipping, which was now at the mercy of Japanese air attack, weakening an already untenable defensive position.

The loss of HMS *Prince of Wales* and *Repulse* on 10 December by the Genzan Air Group – an aircraft and airbase garrison unit of the Imperial Japanese Navy Air Service – further established Japanese supremacy. The fact that the Japanese ground forces had effective close air support from the beginning of their campaign, coupled with superiority in the air above the jungle canopy, meant Japanese ground forces could capture and make good use of Allied airfields for future operations.

On 3 January 1942, fifty-one disassembled Hawker Hurricane Mk IIB fighters, which had originally been en route to Iraq, were diverted to Singapore. Ten were in crates and the rest partially disassembled. They arrived in Singapore along with twenty-four pilots, many of whom were Battle of Britain veterans who had been transferred with the intention of forming the nucleus of five fighter squadrons. The fifty-one aircraft were assembled by the 151st Maintenance Unit in just two days. Of these twenty-one were cleared as being ready for operational service within three days. The aircraft had to be fitted with a bulky dust filter which protruded from beneath the nose. These fighters were initially fitted with the standard eight .303-inch Browning machine-gun configuration, plus an additional four .303-inch Browning machine guns were added to the armament. This increased the firepower of these Hurricane fighters yet the extra weight and drag these extra weapons plus their ammunition added proved detrimental to the aircraft's performance. The Hurricane was notorious for its sluggish rate of climb and the extra guns proved an added hindrance. Its manoeuvrability at altitude was also affected by the weight of the additional armament. The Hurricane was, however, an extremely rugged and stable gun platform and was far superior to the Brewster Buffalo. It had proved itself as a highly efficient bomber killer during the Battle of Britain, and it would live up to its expectations against Japanese bombers. Flying Officer Wright felt optimistic at the news that at least some decent Allied fighter aircraft were now arriving in theatre:

I knew the Hurricane was one of the best fighter aircraft we had; its rate of climb was not as good as say that of a Spitfire, nor was its maximum altitude as good either. Yet, when you compare it with the Brewster Buffalo which we had been flying, it at least looked like a fighter aircraft and its performance was far superior to that of the Buffalo. I felt that if we had enough of these Hurricanes, then we at least stood a better chance against the Nakajima Ki-43s and the Zeros.

The problem was they added extra machine guns to the aircraft which I felt was not necessary. Eight machine guns were adequate for knocking down any Japanese fighter, even the Zero. The Japanese bombers were harder to shoot down though and could take a lot of punishment from rifle-calibre bullets. The .303-inch Browning machine gun fired the same 7.7x56R cartridge as used in our standard Lee Enfield rifles and Bren light machine guns. It would have been better had they fitted two or four 20mm Hispano or Oerlikon cannon to these aircraft. The Hispano and the Oerlikon fired much larger 20x110 ammunition including armour-piercing and explosive shells. I suggested their use on more than one occasion only to be rebuffed by those 'snobs' higher up the ladder who thought they knew better than me. I was told the necessary modifications could not be carried out in the field without compromising the operational status of the aircraft, and it would prove yet another logistical issue.

The tropical air filters which had to be added beneath the nose of these aircraft also affected performance. You can't go bolting on things like this if they were never an original part of the specification as it affects the aerodynamics in ways you would not expect. A Hurricane without these big air scoops beneath their noses performed differently to those fitted with them. If you haven't taken this issue into account, then you find the aircraft responds differently in combat and you can end up in trouble having not accounted for this problem. It's all basic common sense when it comes to aerodynamics.

We were, however, writing the textbook at that time and not reading from it. It was embarrassing; not only had we been caught with our pants down by the Japanese, the Japanese had effectively sneaked up behind us and yanked our pants down to our ankles in full view of the world. It was humbling but I felt we would regain the initiative and we would get better aircraft and we would wipe the Japanese from the air. It was all just a matter of time; setbacks are all a part of warfare, it happens, and you learn, and you come back stronger and better prepared, and that's precisely what we did.

Royal Australian Air Force veteran Robert McGilling has fond memories of the first Hurricane fighters to arrive in theatre:

They were a reassuring presence, for sure; they may not have looked that pretty with that big air filter ducting

53

hanging off their chins but with a good pilot at the controls they would make a difference to the jungle air war. These aircraft had twelve Browning machine guns as opposed to the standard eight. The idea was to adjust the guns so as their combined firepower would converge at a single point and at a set range. Adjustments such as this make a huge difference to the firepower of these machine guns. If they were set up correctly, they would cut a Jap aircraft in two like a rip saw. It was all about the weight of shot of all twelve weapons focused on a certain aiming point ahead of the aircraft. We also had incendiary ammunition which proved highly effective against Japanese aircraft which were known to catch fire very easily. The .303-inch incendiary cartridge had a bullet packed with a phosphorus pellet; this round was designated by a blue painted tip. The armourers would mix incendiary and ball in the ammunition belts. Of course, we would have preferred it if our Hurricanes had been armed with 20mm cannon, but at that time we had to make do with the resources we had been given.

Hikokuru Ishimaru was unfazed by the presence of Hawker Hurricanes in the region:

We knew all about the Hurricane and while it was an excellent aircraft, it did have limitations when compared to our fighters. It carried more machine guns than our Ki-43s but lacked the firepower of our Zeros; it was let down by a slow rate of climb and poor operational altitude. It was also heavier than both the Zero and Ki-43 so we did not feel anxious on their arrival; on the contrary we looked forward to engaging in air combat with them.

Any notion of chivalry between Imperial Japanese Army Air Service (IJAAS pilots) and their Allied counterparts in the air war was also soon dispelled after the first series of air-to-air engagements. A very worrying trend began to make itself immediately apparent – the Japanese tendency to shoot Allied pilots in their parachutes after baling out of their aircraft.

This detested practice became a common occurrence during the air war over Asia. One of the first accounts of this happening was recorded on 17 January 1942, near Bilton Island, some miles off Singapore, and was witnessed by Australian pilot Herb Plenty who recalled:

> I witnessed a Dutch Brewster Buffalo being shot down by Japanese fighters; the pilot was able to get out of his aircraft and I saw his parachute safely deploy. Most of the Japanese fighters turned for home; however, I saw two of them turn back. In what was nothing more than a parting gesture of hate, they dived towards the descending parachute and fired long bursts of gunfire at the Brewster pilot who was swinging helplessly in the canopy rigging. A concerted and immediate growl of rage rose from most of us, conveying our feelings that the Japanese pilots had just perpetrated an act amounting to unfair tactics, treachery and outrageously coarse conduct. Previously, among British and German pilots, an unwritten code of honour, chivalry if you like, assumed that pilots descending by parachute should not be shot at by opposing aircraft. The Japanese served notice that they held no such gentlemanly opinions.

On 31 March 1943, a squadron of United States Army Air Forces (USAAF) B-24 bombers sent to destroy a bridge at Pyinmana, Burma, was attacked by Zero fighters. One B-24 was shot down and its occupants, including Second Lieutenant Owen J. Baggett, baled out. While the B-24 crew were descending, they were machine-gunned by the Japanese fighters. Two of the B-24 crewmen were killed, and Lieutenant Baggett was wounded in the arm. He decided the only possible way to survive would be to play dead, hanging limp in his harness, hoping the Japanese would leave him alone. One Japanese Zero, however, circled and approached very close to Baggett to try and ascertain as to whether he was dead. Baggett then raised his Colt Government M1911 pistol and fired four shots into the cockpit, hitting the pilot. The Zero stalled and crashed into the ground. Baggett became a legend in his own right for being the only person to down a Japanese aircraft and claim a kill with an M1911 pistol.

Having read a catalogue of accounts where Japanese pilots shot Allied aircrew while parachuting to safety, I decided to put the question to Hikokuru Ishimaru who explained his theory on the subject:

> It was again all a question of honour for us: baling out of your aircraft once shot down was considered an act of surrender and surrender was shameful in Japanese military culture of the day. If a man surrendered even his aircraft, even if it were a ball of flames and he knew death would take him within just a few seconds, to bale out of that aircraft was considered an act of cowardice and shame. If we were shot down and facing death, we were told that we should either try and ram an enemy aircraft or crash our aircraft into a target on the ground if one was available. If neither scenario arose, we should die honourably for our emperor and our nation. This was by no means an obligation, as pilots were valuable to our military, but a man's individual honour could be judged by his last minutes in such a situation; his path to an ultimate greatness was assured by those actions. Yes, it may be very difficult for you to understand this way of thinking, but this is how it was at that time. It all seems madness when one looks back on it. I think our whole military philosophy frightened the Allies. In that sense was it not effective?

I then presented the ageing Japanese air force veteran with the question of war crime and murder, and whether such actions were indeed murder in its purest form and a war crime:

> Again, understanding that this was our military philosophy is paramount to considering if such actions were criminal or not. I did not shoot any Allied pilot in his parachute, I could have done on more than one instance, but I did not. That was my personal choice; other pilots of our fighter groups did not share that view and would dispose of any surviving enemy to prevent them returning to battle against the Japanese forces.

I felt that the old man was dodging the real issue here, his slightly cryptic response to my questions perhaps in some way betraying him, that there was an element of guilt in this man's soul after all. I left it there and decided it was best not to push the issue any further, at least for the time being. Upsetting him, I felt, would be entirely pointless and might jeopardize the whole proposed literary project.

During those early months of the Japanese conquest, the skies above the jungles of Asia belonged to the Japanese. The balance of power would steadily shift with certain lessons having been learned, yet learning the lessons proved a costly endeavour for the Allied air forces who had effectively been taken back to school by the Japanese in more ways than one. However, the Allied air forces would return stronger and more aggressive and would prove an equally unforgiving foe.

Chapter 5

Asian Supermen

In December 1941 the Japanese Empire began its assault on the British territories of Hong Kong, Malaya, Singapore and Burma. The Imperial Japanese Army Air Force (IJAAF) had secured air superiority over what was a rapidly expanding battlefront, soon dispelling any preconceived western notions that the Japanese were an inferior enemy.

In the early hours of 4 December 1941, Lieutenant General Tomoyuki Yamashita, the commander of the Japanese Twenty-Fifth Army, gazed up at the sky, as twenty maritime transports steamed out of Samah harbour on the morning tide. Yamashita noted that the sun was up, yet the moon had not yet set at that moment and took the joint presence of these two heavenly entities as an omen, a symbol of good fortune for the Japanese campaigns that lay ahead. Yamashita was described as a hardened military man through and through, resolute, stern and quick tempered. He was a man who accepted no excuses for failure, where failure was not an option. In this sense he was the embodiment of the Japanese military philosophy of the time, and a man totally dedicated to the service of his emperor. It was said that morning outside his cabin aboard the *Ryujo Maru*, after marvelling at the heavens that Yamashita had penned a short poem to mark what he felt was an occasion of great importance, yet sadly the words of his composition were never recorded for posterity.

General Yamashita's invasion force set off from the island of Hainan off the south coast of China on a 1,100-mile voyage across open sea. Japanese military planners had predicted the voyage to take around four days. The armada aiming to land at three specific invasion beaches on the eastern shores of the Kra Isthmus, a narrow neck of land where southern Thailand bordered northern Malaya. The force would steam down the South China Sea, where it would then rendezvous with an escort of Japanese naval ships off the southern tip of Indochina.

As a combined force, the armada would then enter the Gulf of Siam, veering off sharply to the west and south until it arrived at the proposed invasion beaches on the far side of the gulf. All was going well for General Yamashita at this time and fortune, it seemed, was smiling upon him and his command.

British Far East Command Headquarters (BFECH) in Singapore had been alerted to the Japanese activity when a Lockheed Hudson light bomber on patrol from the RAF airfield at Kota Bharu in the north of Malaya spotted the Japanese force. The RAF Hudson flew alongside the Japanese ships, its crew reporting back their observations. The Hudson had to break off when Japanese fighter aircraft appeared. It promptly came under attack from the Japanese fighters but was able to make good its escape. General Yamashita was now aware of the fact that the Japanese ships had been sighted: their size, course and speed would have all been reported back to BFECH, and that some form of reaction could thus be expected. Yet luck appeared again in the form of worsening weather. The heavy rainstorms that swept in closed down visibility, making aerial reconnaissance impossible.

As planned, at 1900 hours, Yamashita's convoy swung north, as if heading into the Gulf of Siam, and, when it changed course again the next morning, the sky was still overcast and the weather had deteriorated; however, at 1010 hours, Yamashita received a signal from Vice-Admiral Ozawa that landing operations could go ahead as planned.

The landing most affected by the poor weather conditions was at Koto Bharu, where Major General Takumi was in command. A signal relayed by the flagship indicated that although waves were now up to three feet high, conditions on the whole were good. During the early hours of the 8th, Yamashita learned that just before midnight the three transports carrying Takumi and his men had anchored offshore with their naval escort. What he was not informed of was the fact that they were 2,000 yards to the south of their correct position and directly opposite the guns of the 8th Indian Brigade. Chikao Oshimaru, a private soldier serving with Takumi's force, recalled what happened next:

> There was some dull, ghostly moonlight from over the sea to the east. There was a stern wind blowing at the time and the waves had increased to six feet. This was at the limits acceptable for such a landing at sea to take place; it was

not ideal. Our main problem came from the lowering of the landing craft, as they began to swing violently due to the bad conditions. Then, once on the water, the craft would be dragged briefly away from the side of the ship then slammed back against it. It was terrifying for those of us in those landing craft. Men were screaming out in the darkness, fearful that they would be crushed to death. Men were falling overboard, and the engineers had the job of fishing them out of the water. Some never made it; they just vanished in the darkness – even though we all had lifejackets on, we had so much equipment to carry. Because of the bad weather it took much longer for the first wave of our landing craft to be launched than was originally expected.

We were also attacked from the air by the English and General Takumi's vessel, the *Awajisan Maru*, was hit by a bomb. As we headed into the shore, arranged in four lines, for a time all I could hear was the noise of our craft's engines, but then the unmistakeable crack of rifle fire which was soon joined by artillery and machine guns. It appeared we were facing an enemy who was not only prepared but in strong numbers too. There was some concern expressed by the commanders, one calling for the operation to be aborted. General Takumi would have faced all manner of logistical issues with such a command and so he refused to abort the operation and gave the order to push on. General Takumi had some near misses – he was almost killed by the bomb that hit his vessel and command headquarters; as his ship sank, he called for another transport ship, but then, typical of his character, he decided to head straight for the shore into the danger.

There was carnage initially; many of our soldiers were cut down by machine-gun fire, men were struggling to keep their balance as they made their way to the shore under fire. The waves rushed in, rolling you over and off your feet and it was a desperate struggle to get out of the water. Our commanders were exceptionally brave though, rushing on towards the enemy positions among the palm trees and calling us all to follow, which, of course, all of us who safely made it to dry land did. We then began to rapidly outflank our enemy, getting around the back of him using rifles, bayonets, and grenades. It was not difficult or tough, but just how we had been trained and it came naturally. I made my first ever kill of the war with my bayonet. I stabbed as I had done so many times in training: the bayonet was effective as it cut through the Indian's chest, exiting his back between the shoulders. I withdrew my bayonet and kicked my enemy over and he fell backward like a drunken man staggering from a bar. I just thought, 'Yes, that is one less enemy we have to face.' Another enemy was crouching behind a palm with his rifle. He did not see me. I stabbed him from behind with all my strength and again the point of the bayonet came out the other side. He did not know what had got him; he was dead within seconds. All around I could hear my comrades engaged in their own hand-to-hand fighting with the enemy, many of whom had begun to run away. We had terrified them with our unwillingness to retreat. Any we captured were quickly killed; there were few prisoners taken at that instance. We had no pity for the enemy; they had killed men I knew, men who were my friends and not just fellow Japanese. How could they expect mercy from us when we died as warriors? I saw some enemy with their hands raised in surrender. I thought to myself, 'How could they ever face their families or leaders again having committed an act of such shame?'

Yes, in that battle we showed the enemy that we were far from the little yellow men with glasses and gold teeth that they held in such contempt. This was their lesson – that the Japanese soldier was ready for anything they could throw at us. We were ready to die, we were proud to give our lives and that was the difference: a western enemy does not wish to die, he is selfish by the way he will desert his comrades and run; he just wants to live.

A number of soldiers of the 8th Indian Brigade were captured by the invading Japanese yet were not subject to any of the immediate trademark brutality as suffered by some. One of those captured Indian soldiers was Pardeep Gahor, who recalled:

> The Japanese knew we were frightened, and they made us a simple offer. A high-ranking Japanese officer came to us and he told us, 'You are fellow Asians. We have showed you mercy and we ask you to take up arms in the struggle against your colonial masters alongside the Japanese Empire. You can join us as brothers and become part of our Greater Asian Prosperity Sphere. You can fight those who have enslaved you and free yourselves of British rule and regain your respect and honour. If you join us in battle against the colonialists, together we shall defeat them.' This was the offer placed before us, and I understood that to decline the offer would be signing my own death warrant. I told them, 'Yes, I will join you.' Did I feel any shame for doing so? Not at that time I didn't, as I wanted to see my family again. If joining the Japanese meant that when all this was over, I could return home to a free India, then I was happy to go along with it.
>
> Yes, looking back they [the Japanese] were very clever in preying upon our fears and insecurities, yet I knew in a sense they were right. We were effectively slaves in our own country; many of us enjoyed no respect under British colonial rule. We had been reduced to being servants of the rich white people, and we resented that deeply at that time. So, yes, I agreed to fight with them and was spared. You ask what became of those who declined the Japanese offer. Some went to prisoner of war camps while some were killed. I heard stories of the Japanese bayoneting those who defied them after tying them to trees. I was later given the honour of being a guard at one of the British prisoner of war camps. The Japanese treated me differently – they treated me as an equal.

General Yamashita was aboard his ship in Singora harbour, having arrived at 0035 hours. He noted there was no opposition and his forces disembarked in parade order. Yamashita went ashore himself at 0520 hours. One of his staff recorded in a diary the moment they arrived on land: 'General Yamashita appeared very satisfied overall with how the operations had gone. We ourselves had encountered no opposition. General Yamashita stood momentarily gazing about himself; he was a leader who seldom smiled, yet here I was by his side and I saw him smiling as he looked about taking in the scene. It was a good feeling.' Yamashita himself recorded the following in his diary:

0800 hours: Entered the Governor's residence and ordered that the police were to be disarmed.
1300 hours: Succeeded in reaching a compromise agreement with the Thailand government.
2300 hours: Formalities completed allowing us to pass through Thailand.

The so-called 'compromise agreement' mentioned by Yamashita was somewhat of a euphemism: the Siamese government were left with few options other than to submit to the demands of the Japanese, or see their country destroyed. Yamashita was a man who compromised with no one, so in this sense the compromise he mentions in his writings was merely a blunt demand to the Thai government.

The gateway was now open for the Japanese advance into Malaya. Colonel Tsuji, Operations Staff Officer of the Japanese Twenty-Fifth Army, had his vehicles filled with troops disguised as civilian refugees and Siamese troops, and rushed them over the border to seize vital bridges before the British could destroy them.

General Yamashita at that moment had received the news that the massed Japanese air assault on Pearl Harbor had been a devastating success. Seen to smile upon receipt of the news, he could now relax to a degree and focus on the campaigns ahead, confident that naval supremacy in the Pacific now lay with the Japanese. One of his staff officers wrote:

General Yamashita stood bolt upright and looked at us, curled up his lip in a gesture of angry defiance, nodded his head and then smiled at us. The implications of our victory over the Americans at Pearl Harbor gave us total control in the air over the whole of the Malayan peninsula and Singapore. We could go forward unmolested by the enemy, and we would hit them harder than they had ever been hit before – of this we were all highly confident. When General Yamashita smiled, you understood that something of greatness had occurred. We congratulated one another; it was a moment of great victory.

The British had in every sense been complacent about the Japanese activity: muddle, confusion and embarrassing indecision ensued. The Japanese appeared like jungle ants, swarming and thriving on the incompetence of their British enemy. British intelligence had failed in many areas to assess the true Japanese objectives. By the time Japanese intentions were fully realized, it was too late. To compound matters, disaster was to befall the Royal Navy. On 8 December, the new Commander-in-Chief Eastern Fleet, Admiral Sir Tom Phillips, left Singapore with the battleships *Prince of Wales* and *Repulse* plus four destroyers. Japanese reconnaissance aircraft spotted the naval force on the evening of the 9th and picked them up again the following morning. Soon after noon on the 10th, both capital ships were attacked by Japanese torpedo bombers and were sunk. Many of the crew of these ships were saved, but the Commander-in-Chief and the captain of the *Prince of Wales* both went down with the ships. The news would come as a heavy blow to the British forces who soon found themselves having to retreat from the Japanese onslaught pushing towards Singapore. Vital airfields had to be abandoned as these were soon overrun by the Japanese who utilized them for their own aircraft.

It was said that Singapore should be defended to the last man. Regarded by the British as the 'Gibraltar of the East', Singapore was the major British military base in the region and was the key to British imperial interwar defence planning for South-East Asia and the South-West Pacific. The Japanese forces under General Yamashita were tearing a path through Malaya towards this prize jewel in the British crown. Yamashita himself soon earned the nickname of the 'Tiger of Malaya'.

The whole Japanese strategy for the Malaya campaign was very simple. From Singora and Pattani, Japanese forces would strike westward across the Kra Isthmus – less than 100 miles wide at that point – then move southward into Malaya and down the west coast, thus bypassing the mountain range central to the peninsula. Coincident with the thrust down the west coast, where Malaya's best roads had been constructed, a secondary drive would be made from Kota Bharu down the east coast. Near the tip of the peninsula, the two forces would converge for an assault on Singapore, which was considered the main objective of the Malayan campaign. Success was everything to the Japanese at this stage who would gain a huge propaganda and psychological victory over the British if Singapore could be taken.

The British forces opposing the Japanese in Malaya found themselves at an immediate and dangerous disadvantage. Short on tanks, artillery and communications equipment, primarily due to being afforded low priority for military materiel, the British Army's tactical thinking for the Malayan campaign was also rooted in the European model. The troops themselves were neither conditioned nor trained for fighting in the jungle and were woefully ill equipped for the task.

The Japanese noted that the British forces were 'laden as if mules, with much unnecessary equipment such as packs, haversacks, blankets, gas masks and rations, the majority of which was supplied in bulky tin cans'. It was certainly no way for any soldier to go into battle. Akihara Koto recalls:

> Mobility is always an army's best weapon. The British could not move quick enough to meet our threats for many reasons. One of them was the amount of equipment they carried with them on their person. Tin cans of rations, for example: if you have even four or five of these cans in your pack, they are a serious burden especially in the jungle. In comparison we carried very little; we carried what was required for the operation at hand. When we marched, we carried enough food, usually just a few balls of rice. We often flavoured the rice balls with pickles and dried seaweed. Our weapons and clothing were lightweight and, most importantly, the jungle was nothing new to us. The greatest difference for us Japanese forces was the fact that we did not fight the jungle – we fought the enemy within it. It was something of a saying in our army that if you fight the jungle and the enemy at the same time, your time is wasted and you will die. In the jungles of Malaya, we developed a

whole new way of military thinking that all armies after the war would have to master; it was unique.

Even prior to the fall of Kota Bharu, the residents of Singapore were to receive a taste of what was to come. At 4.30 a.m. of 8 December, while Japanese forces poured ashore up north, seventeen Japanese Navy bombers roared in to attack Singapore's airfields. Some of the Japanese bombs fell onto the highly populated areas of central Singapore. The city, by habit, was still lively and well-lit at the time of the attack, subsequently casualties were high. Some 200 people, mainly Chinese merchantmen and Sikh night watchmen, were killed and injured, and numerous buildings were destroyed.

Quite astonishingly, an English businesswoman who was living in a flat above her shop watched in horror from her flat window as a Japanese bomb flattened a store down the road. Frantically, she telephoned the police informing them, 'There's an air raid going on; why doesn't somebody put out the lights?' The voice at the other end of the line retorted in a sarcastic tone, 'It's only a practice' to which the woman replied, 'Well, tell them they are overdoing it then!'

The city was totally unprepared for the attack. Singapore's anti-aircraft gunners were so inexperienced that the British were reluctant to send up their night fighters for fear that they would be shot down by their own side. The civilian defence offices were left unmanned – only after the attack was over were the sirens sounded and a blackout considered. The keeper of the keys to the city's master switches for the lights could not be found, and so the city remained awash with light throughout the bombing raid.

Many of the British residents in Singapore still possessed the arrogant attitude that this attack was just a fluke, that Singapore was an impregnable fortress in much the same way as Gibraltar. This privileged colonial elite thought it preposterous that the Japanese could pose a threat to what amounted to more than a century of white rule. In the wealthy whites-only clubs of Singapore, much of the conversation reflected the complacent attitude that many wealthy Britons had become accustomed to. They would say that Japanese ships and aircraft were inferior to those possessed by the western powers, and that Japan's small-calibre weapons couldn't even kill a man. They also discussed the physical ineptitude of the Japanese soldier, sailor and airman, convinced that due to the epicanthic fold which gave his eyes that slanted appearance, he could neither see very well nor shoot straight due to impaired vision. It was one of the Second World War's most astonishing episodes where the myths regarding Japanese inferiority would be laid to rest forever.

General Yamashita had estimated that he could capture Singapore in one hundred days. To the surprise of the Japanese forces, the execution of this goal took just seventy days. Malaya's rugged jungle terrain suited the Japanese ideally in the tactical sense. Although Malaya's road networks were somewhat limited, when they came upon a British position, the Japanese would send in their tanks to storm it. Following close behind were Japanese infantry with fixed bayonets. The idea was simple yet deadly: if the tanks were halted, the infantry would then take up the attack to storm the enemy position. If encountering a roadblock, the Japanese infantry would simply slip into the jungle undergrowth or mangrove swamps alongside the road, forming into small groups of five to ten men; they would then fan out around the enemy's flanks then appear right behind the enemy position. In mangrove swamps the Japanese soldiers would jump from tree root to tree root until clear, the idea to create as much noise as possible, convincing the enemy that they were encountering a superior enemy force. The tanks could then take advantage of the confusion wrought by the 'noise-makers', as they were known, by attacking the bewildered enemy. British reinforcements marching in columns on the roads were captured in this manner. Bicycles were also used by Yamashita's troops to aid their mobility. When the tanks moved forward the Japanese infantry often rode up ahead on bicycles to reconnoitre the road. Then once the enemy had been routed from their position, the cyclists would peddle furiously to outpace their tanks and maintain pressure upon retreating enemy units. Utilizing these same tactical principles over and over again. the Japanese steadily routed all before them en route to Singapore.

By 31 January 1942, Singapore was isolated and under a state of siege – merely the symbol of a receding empire. In the city anything that was felt could be of use to the Japanese enemy was set ablaze. The reek of burning rubber as supplies were destroyed to prevent it falling into enemy hands permeated the air. The thick black acrid smoke which blanketed the streets made Singapore ever more the funeral pyre of British colonial rule.

At 11 p.m. on Friday 8 February, a violent thunderstorm broke in the skies above Singapore, as 440 Japanese artillery pieces began shelling the city. General Yamashita had insisted throughout on maintaining relentless pressure upon the British, and was expending the last of his ammunition as if his supplies were inexhaustible. Using the massive artillery bombardment as cover, the first wave of Japanese troops embarked for the mangrove swamps on Singapore's north-western shoreline. The defenders here were hastily formed Australian battalions fresh from their homeland with no combat experience. The Japanese soon swept them aside using the same tactics that had served them so well all through the Malayan campaign. Terror and death fell upon the unfortunate Australians from all sides. Many fled into the labyrinth of the mangrove swamps, with units becoming separated and lost.

At dawn next morning, a gunner signaller at Tengah Airfield north of Singapore Town observed some of the surviving Australian forces in flight. He recorded the following:

> They came moving at half-trot, panic-stricken. Most of them were dressed in nothing other than issue shorts; few of them were not wearing their boots and most of the men's feet were cut to ribbons as a result. They had discarded their weapons and ammunition and were in a blind state of panic and babbling incoherently. They had been reduced to a rabble; they were utterly terrified from their experience.

Attempting to locate Australian veterans of this action proved almost an impossibility. However, I was lucky, through a family friend who immigrated to Australia many years ago, to make contact with Travis Freeman, whose grandfather fought against the Japanese in the war. He told me the following:

> My grandfather was certainly in the area of your interest, yet he would never speak about what happened. Only after his death did my grandmother tell me some of what had happened to him. He told her that the Japanese attacked them like wild animals. Most men flee or go to ground when fired on, but the Japanese did not do this; they just kept coming at you. It was hard for him to understand their mentality; they came at you screaming with rifles and bayonets and some with short-bladed swords raised above

their heads, hacking and chopping at anything in their path. They cut men down in this manner and he said he saw one Japanese raise his sword and chop a man just below his waist cutting him into two pieces. He admitted they were unprepared and just ran for their lives. He said they stumbled through the darkness, their legs snaring on tree roots and crashing into deep water, thrashing a way through to escape almost certain death. Later after the escape, his feet and legs were in a terrible shape. He had ripped off toenails on the roots of mangrove trees, his shins were grazed almost to the bone in places and thorns had ripped his skin all over his body. All those who had fled were in a similar state. Most were given a telling-off for losing their weapons and ammunition, as the enemy would now have them. They were thoroughly dejected, and I put this down to the reason why he would never talk about it. There were many things he refused to tell even my grandmother. As you know, our forces did fight back after reorganizing things, and I know many did not take many Japs alive. There was so much hate for the Japs they often killed them on the spot rather than take them prisoner; that I do know from other stories I have heard.

By noon of Friday 8 February, a force of around 23,000 Japanese troops was advancing on Buckit Timah, a 600-foot feature that dominated the island. The British counterattacked, yet this soon stalled when again British communications failed and broke down. Over the four days that followed, Japanese forces repaired the causeway across Johore Strait and began to move their tanks across.

By this stage Singapore Town was in a terrible state of ruin from round-the-clock aerial bombardment. The streets were tangled with downed electrical cables, shattered telephone poles, overturned trams and vehicles of all description. The streets were also strewn with the unclaimed bodies of the dead that became bloated in the heat, exasperated further by the fires which had broken out due to the bombings. Sometimes a corpse would become so bloated with gas it would explode. It was a grim picture that few could ever have imagined befalling a place once referred to as the 'Jewel of the Far East'.

The worst horrors were yet to come for the inhabitants as more than a million of its citizens were forced back into an area of just three square miles, where half that number had lived in peacetime.

The island's water supply was rapidly running out: for every six gallons pumped into the city's reservoirs, five gallons were lost due to damaged pipes and conduits. Law and order soon broke down under such circumstances and army deserters shamefully went on a rampage of looting. These looters entered wrecked bars and drank them dry. Becoming increasingly belligerent, they then ransacked shops, taking cigarettes and food items in a futile if selfish attempt in preparing for the collapse of the city.

Singapore and the terror that the Japanese had instilled in the trapped populace would become the hallmark of the Japanese military stamp on the Far East. The much-maligned 'little yellow men' were now regarded as the 'Asian supermen' who had managed to defeat what was a major power in a battle that lasted from 8–15 February 1942.

Chapter 6

Singapore and Surrender

The fall of Singapore, Britain's 'Gibraltar of the East', was the culmination of the decisive campaign of the Japanese Empire over that of the British Empire in the Second World War. The Japanese had overcome a numerically superior enemy through a rapid campaign where the use of asymmetrical warfare had really proved a valuable asset. It would be the greatest military defeat in the history of the British Empire, something that led one British Army officer to remark: 'The Generals of our once proud Empire will be choking on their cognac and cigars for decades to come over this quite embarrassingly bad military debacle. To be beaten or rather convinced we had lost the battle by nothing more than little yellow men on bicycles is a preposterous concept.'

General Yamashita would later admit that Singapore had been a bluff, a military gamble when he recalled:

> My attack on Singapore was a bluff – a bluff that worked. I had 30,000 men and was outnumbered more than three to one. I knew that if I had to fight for long for Singapore, that I would be beaten. That is why the surrender had to be at once. I was very frightened all the time that the British would discover our numerical weakness and lack of supplies and force me into what would have been disastrous street fighting.

There was an excess of arrogance on the part of the British regarding the military capabilities of the Japanese and their ability to take Singapore. One British Army officer stationed in Singapore reflected the attitude of the time regarding the threat posed by the Japanese when he remarked: 'I do hope we are not getting too strong in Malaya, because if so, the Japanese may never attempt a landing.' It was an idiotic proclamation, defying all notions of the seriousness facing the British forces on Singapore Island at that critical time. Yet it was a reflection of the attitude towards the Japanese that many would later regret.

As the Japanese troops attacked through the peninsula, they were ordered to take no prisoners, as theses would slow up the Japanese advance. A pamphlet issued to every Japanese soldier involved in the campaign was brutally stark and read: 'When you encounter the enemy after landing, think of yourself as an avenger coming face to face at last with his father's murderer. Here is a man whose death will lighten your heart.' The text of this pamphlet was sadly indicative of the behaviour of the Japanese military throughout the war.

The British commander of the Allied force in Singapore was Lieutenant-General Arthur Percival. At his disposal were 90,000 British, Indian and Australian troops which should have been more than adequate to have met the Japanese threat had they been allocated correctly. The British were convinced that the Japanese attack would come via invasion from the sea, therefore no provision was made for an attack materializing through the jungle around Singapore. Most of the large-calibre artillery pieces were pointing out to sea when the attack came. Another more pressing issue was that few of Percival's men had experienced combat.

At the Battle of Jitra on 11 December 1941, Percival's soundly beaten forces were forced into a retreat, closely pursued by Japanese troops on bicycles. Any wounded soldiers encountered by the Japanese were killed on the spot. Those Allied soldiers who surrendered were also murdered in an instant. One group of Australians who had surrendered to the Japanese were promptly herded together, had petrol poured over them and were set alight; the men burned to death as the Japanese looked on gleefully. Any locals suspected of aiding the Allied forces were also murdered. Usually the men were taken away and bayoneted while the women were repeatedly raped before being killed. Often the corpses were mutilated which became something of a Japanese trademark.

By 31 January 1942, the Allied forces had withdrawn across the causeway that separated Singapore from Malaya in readiness for a last stand. General Percival spread his forces along a seventy-mile line – the entire coastline of Singapore Island – but made the error of overestimating the strength of the Japanese, and by stretching his own had greatly reduced their effectiveness.

On 8 February, the Japanese attacked across the Johor Strait. Most Allied soldiers were too far away to have any influence on the outcome of the battle. Some 23,000 Japanese soldiers attacked Singapore, and, in scenes reminiscent of their conduct in China, shot, bayoneted and bludgeoned their way through anything which stood in their path. Civilian men, women and children were all slaughtered without an ounce of mercy. Perhaps one of the most infamous incidents was the attack on the Alexandra Military Hospital. When the Japanese burst into the hospital building they embarked upon a frenzy of rape, murder and mutilation. Patients were shot or bayoneted in their beds, and even patients on operating tables undergoing surgery were bayonetted. In one particular incident with a sedated patient on an operating table, the Japanese killed the surgeons and nurses and then left the patient on the table, the idea being that when the patient came to, he would discover to his horror that his amputated leg had only been partially repaired. Akihara Koto recalls the battle for Singapore as if it were yesterday:

Our forces had subjected Singapore to a heavy bombardment as a preparatory measure prior to our attack. Landings took place on the north-west of the island, because at that point the Strait of Johore is narrowest, so you look for the quickest possible way to get across and never the longest; it is all common sense. We knew that there were Australian forces holding the area [Australian 22nd Infantry Brigade], yet during the cover of darkness on the night of 8 February we were able to cut through undefended sections. Twenty-four hours after we had landed, a second landing force made its way from between the causeway and the mouth of the Kranji River, this area also being held by Australians [27th Infantry Brigade].

By dawn of 10 February our forces occupied much of the north-west of Singapore. It felt good to be that close to our objective, which is what we had come all this way for. Yet, with hindsight, it had not taken us long. In fifty-five days, we had pushed 550 miles, with just two divisions. We had no artillery support and relied upon our own initiative under a sturdy commander and we used the jungle to our advantage whereas the Allied soldiers didn't like going into the jungle, so it was very easy. I was looking forward to being in Singapore. I wanted to bath in one of those rich colonials' houses and maybe sleep in one of their beds; dreams like these made us ferocious in the fighting. We fought very hard against sometimes very brave Allied soldiers. I saw some of them run while others tried to hold their ground and continue to fight us. Our idea was to get close enough, fire shots from our rifles and then throw a grenade to finish them. Further resistance was met with the points of our bayonets.

I asked Koto how he dispatched wounded enemy troops or those who had surrendered. The elderly Japanese gentleman took a very deep breath and exhaled before offering his reply. It was as if he were contemplating the answer to some question that he had grown fed up with over the years since 1945.

People wish to know: did I kill a wounded man or a man trying to surrender to us? The answer is yes and no. There were times an enemy would surrender and we would quickly search him then push him towards the rear. The forces in the rear then made the decision whether to shoot the prisoner or keep him alive for some other purpose. Prisoners were shot on orders from above; these were orders from our highest command and our duty was not to argue or contemplate the morals of their actions. We had to act and do as we were told. A good soldier follows orders without asking questions even if he does not necessarily agree with them in principle. Taking prisoners and dealing with wounded enemy were not our concern at all; our concern was to keep pushing forward, keep the momentum going and take Singapore. It all had to be done quickly under the strictest orders from General Yamashita himself. General Yamashita did not issue the order personally to kill Allied wounded and prisoners – this order had already been given to us before we had even approached Singapore. So, yes, I had to kill enemy wounded as we could not have dealt with them at that stage and most of them would have later died anyway had we left them where we found them. You ask about the hospital incident. Well, I was not there so I cannot tell you anything different to what you will already know, and I am sure you know all about that. Just because I know about it does not necessarily mean that I agreed with it. A hospital in my opinion should never be attacked; it should be preserved and utilized, and the staff used to help our Japanese wounded as well as the enemy's. It should have been left alone. But you must remember that this is what warfare is like – sometimes you have to do things that you really do not want to do yet are obliged to do.

I asked Koto how he dispatched wounded enemy troops or those who chose to surrender:

I just raised my rifle, took aim at the enemy's head and squeezed the trigger. A wounded or dying enemy lying on the ground, then maybe a thrust with my bayonet or a single shot to the head again. Either way I did the job I had been instructed to do. Had I failed, it would have shown great dishonour, not only to myself as a soldier, warrior, fighting man of the Imperial Japanese Army but also my family back home that before I left told me to do my duty and die if I must.

One British soldier named Leonard Baynes reminisces coldly on the battle for Singapore:

We lost that battle due to the military hierarchy and its outdated thinking and gross complacency. We had some big guns on Singapore which, had they been mobile, could have caused the Japs significant problems. These guns had been sighted in fixed positions pointing out to sea; nobody ever thought of an attack coming down the Malayan peninsula and into Singapore that way. They should have considered this and other options, but they didn't. When the Japs arrived, it was firstly from the air, bombing the shit out everything really, quite indiscriminate it was and typical of their brand of warfare. The reality on the ground was that although we were taking casualties, we were holding our own. I think had we held out and not opted for surrender, we could have pushed them back, but we had civilians trapped in Singapore to consider and their needs and safety was put before Singapore as a whole.

The thing was these Orientals understood the meaning of saving face and what it was all about, yet they displayed little gratitude for it, for the fact we had laid down our arms and had stopped fighting for their sakes. Over the weeks that followed the surrender, Malays in particular would spit on the ground whenever they saw us – that was the contempt they held us in, yet they were to have worse masters than us with the Japs as they soon found out. The Japanese had cut off the water supply to Singapore and there were the worries about disease breaking out due to the dead bodies that lay everywhere. I recall seeing Indian soldiers trying to bury their dead in shallow graves wherever they could. There was little organization and just confusion everywhere and, in the end, you had all these leaderless soldiers heading for the docks in the hope of getting on board one of the ships out of the place.

It is worthy of note at this point that it would be unfair to entirely blame Lieutenant-General Percival for the loss of Singapore. As early as 1936, Major-General William Dobbie, then General Officer Commanding Malaya, commissioned an inquiry as to whether more forces were required on mainland Malaya to prevent the Japanese from establishing forward bases to attack Singapore. Percival, then Chief Staff Officer, was given the task of drawing up a tactical assessment of how the Japanese were most likely to attack. In 1937 Percival's analysis concluded that northern Malaya might become the critical battleground. He stated in his summary that the Japanese were likely to seize the east coast landing sites in Thailand and Malaya in order to capture airfields and achieve air superiority. This could serve as a prelude to further Japanese landings in Johore to disrupt communications northward and enable the construction of another main base in North Borneo.

From North Borneo, the final sea and air assault could be launched against eastern Singapore – in particular the Changi area. Again, it would seem that the lost art of contingency planning along with complacency towards Japanese military capabilities, poor organization, weak leadership and pure inexperience of the men on the ground were to blame for the capture of Singapore rather than any single decision taken by Percival himself.

When Percival was promoted to acting lieutenant-general in April 1941, and appointed General Officer Commanding Malaya, he expressed concerns, with a sense of foreboding about this command, that

> in going to Malaya I realized that there was a double danger either of being left in an inactive command for years if war did not break out in the East, or if it did, of finding myself involved in a pretty sticky business with the inadequate forces which are usually to be found in the distant regions of our Empire in the early stages of a war.

After a week of bitter fighting on Singapore Island, General Percival held his final command conference at 9 a.m. on 15 February in the Fort Canning 'Battle Box', the HQ Malaya Command bunker. The Japanese were at that stage already in occupation of approximately half of Singapore and it was clear that the island would soon fall. Having been told that ammunition and water would both run out by the following day, General Percival agreed to surrender to the Japanese. The Japanese at that point were running low on artillery ammunition, but Percival did not know this. Had he been aware of this factor he may have made the decision to fight on.

The Japanese issued instructions that General Percival himself should march with a white flag to the old Ford Motor Factory in Bukit Timah where a meeting had been convened to negotiate the terms of surrender. A Japanese officer of General Yamashita's staff recalled that the British general looked 'pale, thin and tired' as he entered the meeting room. Japanese General Tomoyuki Yamashita arrived in his usually brusque manner, his buoyant emotions carefully concealed by his trademark stone-faced expression. There was an awkward silence for some minutes. Another Japanese officer present at the meeting recalled that it was as if the British were trapped within some bad dream, that all of this was not really happening. Their faces were a picture of bewilderment, disbelief at the situation and resignation to defeat. It must have been a humiliation of immense proportions seeing as the British Empire wielded such military power within the world at the time. As a Japanese officer, soldier and servant to our Emperor, I could think of no worse a fate than this. I felt some sympathy for the British general, imagining his position and how he must have been feeling and the thoughts of his people back in England.

The meeting went as follows:

Yamashita:	'I want to hear whether you want to surrender or not; if you want to surrender, I insist on it being unconditional. What is your answer? Yes or no?'
Percival:	'Will you give me until tomorrow morning?'
Yamashita:	'I cannot wait, and the Japanese forces will have to attack tonight.'
Percival:	'How about waiting until 11:30 p.m. Tokyo time?'
Yamashita:	'If that is to be the case, the Japanese forces will have to resume attacks until then. Will you say yes or no?'
Percival:	*no reply*.
Yamashita:	[at this point Yamashita becomes angry with Percival, raises his voice and thumps his fist on the table] 'I want to hear a decisive answer and I insist on an unconditional surrender. What do you say?'
Percival:	'Yes.'
Yamashita:	'All right then. The order to cease fire must be issued exactly at 10 p.m. I will immediately send one thousand troops into the city area to maintain peace and order. Do you agree to that?'

Percival: 'Yes.'

Yamashita: 'If you violate these terms, the Japanese will lose no time in launching a general and final offensive against Singapore City.'

With the surrender documents signed and the proceedings then closed, the fall of Singapore then became a piece of Britain's colonial history it would later rather forget. General Percival, as many other British servicemen, entered into Japanese captivity. Being a senior military officer, he fared far better than the many thousands of lower-ranking British prisoners of war. Many of those British, Indian and Australians who had no option other than to surrender to the Japanese as ordered, were to enter a hell of sadistic barbarism incomprehensible to many in the civilized world. Arthur Hopkins was one of the British soldiers who had to lay down his arms as the terms of the surrender came into force:

It was humiliating. We still had weapons and we still had ammunition for those weapons; we could have fought on, but our senior commanders felt otherwise. It was felt that a major battle occurring in the city would endanger the civilian population, besides the Japs had cut off the water supply. We could have fought on though – we were resourceful enough as individuals to be able to find water somewhere. Some of our units had collapsed into a disorganized rabble – these men were just terrified of the Japs; they had been listening to too many bogeymen stories about them. Yes, the Japs were tough and ruthless little bastards, but we found if you stood your ground and kept firing at them, kept your wits about you and worked as a team, you could deal with them and hold them off. Of course, after the fall of Singapore we had to throw down our Lee Enfields and our ammunition supplies. Some units destroyed their weapons before the Japs arrived by setting them on fire. Some of the artillery was blown up too so the Japs couldn't use it.

When they [the Japanese] arrived, they came in a convoy of trucks with more marching behind them. We stood watching them and as they approached, one Jap jumped off the back of the lorry he was riding on and hit me with the butt of his rifle; he was shouting things at me as I lay curled up on the ground. Some of my pals stepped forward but they soon had guns and bayonets pointing at them. The one that clubbed me to the ground then buggered off. One to one I could easily have beaten and strangled him there and there, but with all his mates around him, what could I or the other Brits do? Apparently, we hadn't bowed to the Japs as they arrived. From then on, we had to bow to every Jap we met, regardless of his rank. I fucking hated them; in fact I totally loathed and despised them, and I still do today. The way they treated us was evil beyond all belief. My only regret was the fact that I got taken prisoner and remained one until the end of the war. I wanted to kill more Japs when we all had to stop killing them; it didn't seem fair to me, but my war ended at Singapore and in some ways I'm bitter I never had the chance to fight back and defeat them. I knew our army would return and I knew we would crush Japan eventually.

Many people have asked me who I blame for Singapore falling to the Japs in the way it did; to that question there is no easy or straightforward answer. I couldn't say that I blame General Percival exclusively – the decisions he made were ones he felt were right at the time under the circumstances. All I can say is that I was glad it wasn't me who had to make the decisions he had to make; it couldn't have been easy. Churchill had issued an order that every man should fight to the last bullet as Singapore was a matter of both British Empire honour and pride. Percival defied that order. One could argue that he saved lives by doing so, but on the other hand those of us who fell into the hands of the Japs, well, thousands of us died, only us lucky ones got through our captivity, but I can tell you it was only just. What kept me going, my own personal motivation for survival, was my parents back home. For their sakes I had to take whatever came, however bad or unpleasant it was and stay alive for them, so that someday I'd go back home to them. That was it.

Another British soldier, Alan Partington, recalled:

> We were treated with no dignity at all in Singapore after the surrender came into effect. The Japs forced us to bow to them; we were beaten up frequently and we had to hand over wedding rings or any other valuables we had on ourselves. I remember a commotion with a mate of mine named Jack Collinson. A Jap wanted his wedding ring and Jack kept trying to reason with the little cunt, saying, 'Look mate, it won't come off.' All the time the Jap was hanging onto the ring, pulling with all his might. He momentarily let Jack's hand go but then called his Jap mates for assistance. They held Jack down on the ground and sliced his fucking finger off to get at the ring. That was the mentality of those who had captured us. I remember thinking, 'Fucking hell boy, you're going to be fucking lucky if you're going to get out of this mess alive.'

At this point Alan began to shake his head in disbelief and became very angry, to the point where we had to stop the interview for a few minutes. I was sitting inside Alan's living room and watched this ageing ex-British soldier as he went out into his backyard and punched a door. I watched him pace like an angry animal in a cage for a few minutes before he came back inside and apologized:

> I'm sorry about that; just that the memories are still very raw of the treatment we received at the hands of those bastards. You wouldn't believe some of the things we saw as we made our way to the prisoner of war camp, as they called it. As they herded us through the jungle, people would come out of their huts to watch. For no reason at all, one Jap ran at a woman with his rifle and bayonet and stuck it in her, forcing her backwards into her hut with the bayonet right through her torso. We could hear the screams and cries of children coming from the hut. When the Jap came out he set fire to the hut. As we were pushed on like cattle, the hut burned. I kept looking back over my shoulder to see if anyone ran out of the hut but no one did. I just couldn't understand that mentality and I still don't today.

Around 80,000 British, Indian and Australian troops were taken prisoner after the fall of Singapore, joining the 50,000 already captured during the earlier phases of the Malayan campaign. What lay in store for these Allied troops now in the hands of the Japanese is perhaps clearer today than it has ever been thanks to the many accounts that have been published on the subject. The Japanese drove their prisoners of war across country with total disregard for their condition, providing their captives with virtually no food or water en route to the many POW camps across the Far East. Alan Partington recalls:

We became so hot, tired and thirsty that we took to drinking our own urine. The Japs wouldn't give us any water and if you tried to ask for water, they'd give you a right beating with their fists, boots and rifle butts. You couldn't keep drinking your own urine; after a while of doing this all you would pass urine-wise was a thick yellowy liquid, which you couldn't possibly drink. When this occurred, it was obvious that your body was beginning to suffer through dehydration.

As the Japs marched us out of Singapore, we just wondered what was in store for us. We knew we were on our way to POW camps where we would most likely be put to work towards the Jap war effort. Put to work was an understatement. They put us to work all right and worked thousands of us to death. If the work as they called it didn't kill you, then the beatings often would. It was never just a slap, kick or a punch but a real hammering. They'd go fucking mad and really smash you up badly. I recall one poor sod, a mate of mine, who was not quick enough to get up and bow to one of the Jap NCOs; by the time that bastard had finished with him, he looked as if he had gone through a car windscreen: his face was unrecognizable, they broke his cheekbone, jaw and had dislodged several of his teeth – he couldn't open his eyes for the swelling for days afterwards. They almost killed him, just for not being quick enough to fucking bow to them. We knew at that point we were all in for a very hard time indeed and survival would depend on a lot of factors.

Statistics for German and Japanese prisoners of war speak for themselves. While the death rate of POWs in German camps was around 4 per cent, in Japanese camps the figure was 38 per cent.

While the British public shared Prime Minister Winston Churchill's consternation over the events leading up to the Japanese capture of Singapore, both Britain and the United States would steadily mobilize into a cohesive force capable of defeating the Japanese. It would be a long hard road to victory in the jungles of the Far East, but nothing other than total victory over the Japanese would be acceptable to the Allies. The prerequisite to defeating the forces of the Empire of Japan on the part of the British lay with the formation of what would become known as the British Fourteenth Army.

Chapter 7

A Quiet Ferocity

From its formation in India in 1943 as part of the 11th Army Group, the British Fourteenth Army was a multinational force encompassing units from Commonwealth countries. It may surprise many that the bulk of the Fourteenth Army consisted of units of the Indian Army, as opposed to the British Army. There were also a significant number of troops of other nationalities from places such as West and East Africa. The Fourteenth Army was without doubt one of the most important ever raised during the conflict that was the Second World War, yet it has since become known as the 'Forgotten Army'. Many of its exploits were overshadowed by those taking place in the European theatre of battle, subsequently it had often been overlooked by the press, leading many of its troops to really believe they had been largely forgotten. The Fourteenth Army for most of its existence was commanded by the enigmatic Lieutenant-General William Slim.

Slim's assessment of the campaign in the Far East was one of a British Army that had been thoroughly outmanoeuvred, outfought and outgeneralled. In his own words he recalled how he had sat and pondered the various solutions required to turn defeat into victory. Upon weighing up the whole situation, he recalled:

> Excuses for failure are of little use; what is required are causes and remedies. Lack of preparation was something which had led to a dreadful muddle. No adequate plan had been in place to deal with a Japanese invasion of Burma, the military separation of Burma from India and subsequent division of operational from administrative control being two of the worst errors. An army whose plan of campaign is founded upon fundamental errors in its organization was destined to fail. Another major problem which occurred out

of the same muddle, was that no serious attempt was made to connect India and Burma by road, so as when Rangoon fell to the Japanese the army in Burma by all intents found itself in an isolated position; attempts at creating a road did transpire but by this time it was too late to effect any change in the military situation. Perhaps the greatest example of the lack of preparation in the forces allocated to defend Burma was the fact that two ill-conceived, hurriedly collected and inexperienced divisions, of which one had been trained and equipped for desert warfare and the other contained a large number of raw and highly unreliable Burmese troops. The reality was these were tragically insufficient to meet well motivated and equipped superior Japanese forces in a country such as the size and topography of Burma. The arrival of Chinese troops may well have readdressed the numerical balance, even beaten the Japanese had they been able to get to the front prior to the fall of Rangoon. Though there were issues with the Chinese troops refusing to obey Stillwell's orders which upon reflection would have proved a negative aspect and almost certainly ensured defeat. The fact we had an inadequate air force put us at an immediate disadvantage to the Japanese. Our air force it seemed were more or less totally eliminated from the campaign and thus unable to exert any influence on its outcome, the Japanese enjoying total air superiority of the skies of the Far East.

These were just tip-of-the-iceberg factors, yet there were many more which had to be considered. General Slim was also particularly scathing of some areas of the Burmese population. He suggested that regardless of the disadvantages the British Army faced militarily, the British were fighting in what should have been a friendly country. It wasn't necessarily so. Slim believed that some five per cent of Burma's population was hostile or unsympathetic to the British, a figure he compares favourably with the number of collaborators in many European countries.

Either way, General Slim had a tough task on his hands, but he was not a man to be put off by such challenges. Through his excellent leadership and the genuine admiration and respect he had for the men under his command, he would succeed in routing the Japanese in Burma. It would not be an easy road to victory; there would be many setbacks, but these would not prove detrimental to total victory.

Kenneth Guthrie, born and bred in the northern English city of Leeds, served as a private soldier with the 2nd Infantry Division of the British Army. He recalled:

> I was a 19-year-old lad back then and for me the Far East was not my first taste of what war was like. I had fought with the BEF [British Expeditionary Force] in France alongside the French Army. We got pretty much hammered by the Germans and were driven back to this small town called Dunkirk. I was one of the lucky ones evacuated back to England, to live to fight another day; not all were so lucky and yes, I lost friends throughout that short disastrous campaign. When we arrived back in England, we were in a sorry state. We had to regroup and reequip ourselves and regain our strength, as they say. For a while there was the threat of invasion from the Germans and we were at readiness for this expected attack which fortunately never came. Of course, when the Japs entered the war in December 1941 with the attack on Pearl Harbor, we saw another disaster steadily unfold with British interests in the Far East. God, those people took a hammering from the Japs and we felt for them, we really did.
>
> It was early 1942 that we heard we were being sent to India, to help defend India from Japanese invasion and to help restore some law and order. The Japs had set panic in the hearts of many Indians and it's hardly surprising, is it, so we were sent across the sea to India, somewhere I'd never been before, only ever seen it in these old encyclopaedia books which my mum and dad used to have, so it was something new, an adventure. We had an excellent commander in General Slim and he was a general who naturally inspired those who served under him, a soldier's general they used to say of him. There was some excitement but also a mixture of fear too. Those of us who had been through France and Dunkirk had an idea of what to expect;

those who hadn't were in for a shock – yes, we used to joke about that among ourselves. When we arrived in India some of us found the climate a struggle: it could be bloody hot and when it rained it was far worse than anything good old Yorkshire could ever throw at you; the rain there came down in buckets and the thunderstorms were something else. Our role at first was taken up with training and internal policing. It wasn't hard at all and for the most part I found the Indians lovely people. Our first real scuffle with the Japs would come at Arakan.

Another soldier of the 2nd Infantry Division was Jaspal Singh. He was a giant of a man even in his old age and certainly one of the most imposing men I had ever met. At six foot tall and seventeen stone, he typified the image of an Indian Sikh as they were portrayed in vintage films – fearless villains charging over sand dunes wielding curved sabres. I often joked with him about this and he always laughed. Of his service during the Second World War, particularly in the fighting against the Japanese in Burma, Jaspal recalled:

The politics of India and the British Empire were not always mutually agreeable, yet in the Second World War we were fighting a common enemy; as part of the then British Empire we fought as British soldiers. As India was our country of birth, we were well acclimatized to the hot humid environment; we knew the land and how to survive off it which were two very important things. The British troops who arrived fresh from the British Isles in particular had a tough time getting used to the heat and humidity of our country, but in all most of them did get used to it as they had to; they couldn't just pack up and go home, there was a job to do.

I had been a soldier for nearly three years prior to the Burma campaign, yet Burma would be the first real combat that I would experience. As part of what became the Fourteenth Army we were a completely new weapon, yet essential to meeting the Japanese threat in Burma. I myself was ready to go and fight the Japanese. Was I afraid of them?

I was not afraid of them in the sense of their physical capability, but certainly in the moral sense I was. I had heard what they had done to captured enemy soldiers and innocent civilians and I was shocked by their cruelty. The Japanese were not an enemy that you wanted to be captured by. With captured Indian troops they would firstly try to convince you to join them, that joining them was the better option. If you then refused, they would torture and kill you. That was the only fear I had of them – being captured and tortured to death, as I would never have joined them, no matter what. There was a new feeling of confidence that we as part of the Fourteenth Army would fight back and defeat the Japanese; there was a lot of guts and a lot of spirit not just among the Indians but the Africans, Nepalese, British and Australians who all fought with the Fourteenth Army.

Former private soldier Mark Rutherford was another 19-year-old who found himself in India as part of the 2nd Infantry Division. With his strong cockney accent and a sense of humour he admitted was often offensive, he was a man I certainly felt at ease with. I found Mark very typical of many of the Second World War veterans I had spoken with over the years. His accent gave that strange sense of assurance that you were in the presence of a practical man who had seen and done a lot throughout his years. He recalled:

God, India ... fucking hell, where do we start with that? [he laughs] Back then India was okay if you were one of those toffs living it up; you know, the high life as we used to call it. It must have been pretty good there. When I arrived, I thought to myself: fucking hell, it's hot here, can't bloody breathe, there's no air movement here – not like standing on the London docks where my old man used to work his knackers off for a charity wage. No, I didn't like it there at first; it was what you'd call very primitive and what with those fucking officers and sergeants barking orders at you all day long – but we were there and had to get used to it pretty quickly because they said the fucking Japs were coming.

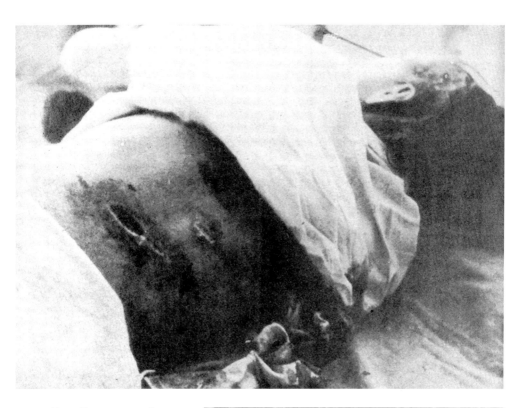

Above: Bayonet wounds found on a child victim of the Nanking Massacre.

Right: Indians secretly despised their white colonial masters.

White colonial extravagance. The opulence many of white colonials indulged in was far removed from the indigenous population of the Far East.

Above left: Akihara Koto. (*Akihara Koto*)

Above right: Tomoyuki Yamashita, the 'Tiger of Malaya'. (*Wikipedia*)

Two Japanese soldiers hitch a ride on the front of a train. (*Taka Ishizawa*)

Bayonet practice with a live victim.

Japanese soldiers in training. (*Taka Ishizawa*)

Above: Japanese soldiers consulting their maps during an exercise. (*Taka Ishizawa*)

Right: Portrait photo of a young Japanese soldier. (*Taka Ishizawa*)

Japanese soldiers move through the jungle.

The much-maligned Brewster Buffalo which was totally outclassed by the Japanese fighters. (*Imperial War Museum*)

The Mitsubishi A6M Zero fighter quickly gained air superiority in the skies of the Far East during the early phases of Japan's war. (*Wikipedia*)

An RAF Spitfire prepares for take-off. (*Wikipedia*)

Field Marshal William Slim, nemesis of the Japanese in the Far East campaign. (*Wikipedia*)

These unfortunate 'comfort women' found themselves as victims of Japanese sexual depravity.

Somewhere in the jungle. (*Author's collection*)

Sergeant Johns (right) relaxes with a friend. Both served in the Fourteenth Army. (*Author's collection*)

Soldiers of the Fourteenth Army somewhere in Burma. Jaspal Singh is seated at front. (*J. Singh*)

Field Marshal Bill Slim (centre) flanked by some of his Fourteenth Army soldiers, Burma. (*Author's Collection*)

Above: British troops pay homage to the fallen. (*Author's Collection*)

Right: Japanese brutality aided the Allied propaganda machine.

Allied aircraft somehwere in the Far East. (*Taka Ishizawa*)

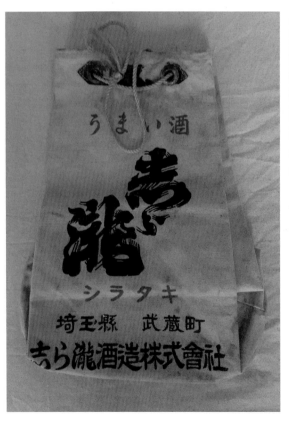

Above: Captured Japanese flag from Burma. (*Author's collection*)

Left: Sake bag. (*Author's collection*)

Japanese occupation currency. (*Author's collection*)

Japanese remains including a bullet-holed helmet. (*Taka Ishizawa*)

Above: A post-war
memorial service to the
fallen, possibly at Kohima.
(*Author's collection*)

Left: A British soldier
of the Fourteenth Army
in tropical uniform.
(*Author's Collection*)

Right: The newspaper headline announcing the execution of General Yamashita.

Below: Japanese soldiers bayoneting Sikh prisoners of war. (*Imperial War Museum*)

The emaciated state of Allied POWs horrified the civilized world. (*Wikipedia*)

Child victims of a Japanese massacre. Hellish scenes such as these were commonplace in all areas of Japanese occupation. (*Wikipedia*)

A Japanese prisoner of war displays the shame and dejection of capture by Allied forces. (*Wikipedia*)

Japanese soldiers giving candy to a Chinese girl. The apprehensive expression on her face tells another story.

Left: All that remained of this victim of the Hiroshima bomb was a shadow on the paving. Many such victims were vapourized in an instant. (*Wikipedia*)

Below: Hiroshima in the wake of the first atomic bomb attack. (*Wikipedia*)

The two atomic bombs that devastated Hiroshima and Nagasaki brought a swift end to the Second World War. Atomic weapons have never been used in a war since. (*Wikipedia*)

Japanese pilot portrait. (*Taka Ishizawa*)

Left: Chi Wong aged 18 in 1947. Chi survived the Nanking Massacre but was sexually abused by Japanese soldiers.

Below: RAF Brewster Buffalo fighters were totally outclassed by their Japanese counterparts. This artwork depicts Buffalo fighters attempting take off under attack from Japanese Ki-54 fighters.

Above: Remains of Japanese troops killed in battle in the jungle.

Right: A Japanese propaganda photo of a Japanese soldier charging with fixed bayonet. This is the memory many Allied servicemen would have of the Japanese soldier.

The kamikaze, unrelenting samurai of the skies. This artwork depicts a Japanese fighter being flown into a US aircraft carrier.

Japanese prisoners of war on their way home. Many appear surprisingly cheerful.

Left: Hideki Tojo at the Japanese war crimes trial in Tokyo. Tojo was found guilty of all charges and was executed by hanging on 23 December 1948. (*Pearl Harbor Visitors Bureau*)

Below: Japanese Emperor Michinomiya Hirohito. A war criminal who escaped the noose. (*Wikipedia*)

We did a hell of a lot of amphibious landing training, getting in boats, jumping out into the water, getting back in boats – drove us fucking mad, it did. After a few months of that, we used to say the Japs would be our mates. I'd never met an Indian or 'coolie' as some of the lads used to refer to them before. I had never even tasted this stuff they called curry until then either. Those Indian soldiers [and civilians] could make a curry out of virtually anything – from a tree to a dead fucking rat, and it was delicious [he laughs]; fuck me; it really was. Throw in a bit of rice and this bread the women often made which was flat circular-shaped stuff, and bloody hell, you were ready to go; it was filling grub, I can tell you. Some of those spices they had – Jesus! they'd blow your arsehole out the next morning when you took a shit. Not all the lads could handle the spice. One complained it felt as if he were shitting a campfire out of his arse the next morning. The Indians found this amusing and so did we, so, yes we soon broke the ice with the Indian lads and some of them would become lads you could depend on with your life – they'd look out for you as much as you would them, proper mates, which we didn't expect at first being culturally different and all that. Our officers used to fuck me off with their attitude towards the Indians though. Officers always came from upper-class, privileged backgrounds and tended to look down on the Indians. On more than one occasion I heard our own officers refer to the Indians as 'wogs', 'fuzzy wuzzies' or 'nig-nogs'. I personally didn't find it amusing at all, but that's how detached some of the officer classes were from us foot sloggers. We didn't call them names though, and we treated them the same way we would want to be treated. The way I saw it we were all soldiers of the Fourteenth Army and we were all on the same side and we all had the same job to do.

The only bit I wasn't looking forward to was going into that fucking jungle. You couldn't see jack shit in there: a Jap could be right by you and you'd never see the little yellow cunt until he stuck his bayonet in your ribcage and by that point it was over. I heard all about their tactics and the methods they used. That's what they were like, right cunning little fuckers and in the jungle it was often very dark, humid, with lots of fucking things crawling around and they seemed to thrive in it whereas we did struggle for a while. We all sensed before long we'd get a crack at the Japs. We had to learn to use the jungle as they had been using it. To not be intimidated by the fact that your jungle camp could be surrounded by the Japs, that they were always nearby – we had to get through that mental challenge and to use the jungle itself to travel through as opposed to the roads which may have ran alongside it. Yes, we all had a lot to learn but learn we did. First blood was Arakan – never heard of the place before in my life; it sounded like something from one of those old Sinbad films. Yes, Arakan was the first taste of battle for our gang.

It was perhaps the greatest tragedy for me personally that Mark would pass away halfway through this project. It was sad that a man who had so much to tell never had the chance to fully contribute and see and hold this book in his hands as he had wanted to.

Gurkha Jaspal Gahor was one of the many friends that Mark Rutherford made during his time in India and Burma. They had remained in contact with one other, regularly attending reunions over the years after the war and it was Mark who put me in touch with this now ageing Nepalese gentleman with a memory as vivid as that of 20-year-old. Talking from his home in Wolverhampton, he recalled:

As you will be aware, the people of Nepal have served Britain for centuries. Our young men aspire to become Gurkha soldiers and serve with the British Army; it is considered one of the greatest of honours for us. I remember when the British first came; many of them were just boys and they had not seen a war and all of its horrors. They didn't like the heat, rain, snakes and spiders and things, and they hated and feared the jungle they would soon have to make their home. For me the jungle was nothing; it was neither an obstacle nor an easy passage. It was as nature made it and adapting to it for me was a natural process from birth.

From a boy I learned how to use the famous kukri knife. I do not understand all the fuss and mythology which surrounds it, as to us it is a tool just like a knife and fork is to many people. You master the ways of using the kukri as our people have for centuries. It is a tool for working, cooking and also for fighting with in war. When I came of age my father gave me my own personal kukri knife, so by the time I became a soldier, my knife was a matter of pride despite the rifle and bayonet I was issued with by the British Army of which I was a part. People used to ask me about my knife. They heard that if I unsheathed it, I would have to draw blood [he laughs] and that this was a Gurkha custom. This is not strictly true as we had to unsheathe our knives to prepare wood cuttings and food, and to sharpen them. Some did believe in this custom that if the knife were drawn unnecessarily then a small nick in the finger to draw blood would be enough. People then ask me if I cut the ears off my Japanese victims and wore them around my neck as trophies. Yes, I cut the ears from the Japanese enemy that I killed in battle but I didn't wear them around my neck [he laughs]. The heat in the tropics would have soon turned them rotten and flies would have infested me, and such a thing would not have been a good idea; your comrades would have complained about you smelling too [he laughs]. People also ask me what it was like to kill a man with the kukri knife. The kukri was always razor sharp, so sharp you could use it to have your morning shave. In a hand-to-hand fight your enemy lunges at you with his bayonet; with one hand you deflect the rifle and with the other you deliver a blow from your kukri which severs his whole arm off, then a strike to the throat which severs his head in one clean movement. Any part of the body which takes a forceful blow from the kukri will be sliced wide open. We had our rifles and bayonets, and these were used many times, but the kukri for us was the true Gurkha weapon and yes, we liked to use our kukris whenever the opportunity arose. People ask about the trophy collecting and the removing of ears from an enemy soldier. It was perhaps one way of confirming you had killed and gave our officers an idea of how many Japanese we had killed altogether. Though not everyone cut off an ear of a dead Japanese.

Gurkha Jaspal Gahor spoke with an almost quiet ferocity of the Japanese enemy he would soon be confronting in the jungles of Burma:

They were a bad enemy; they raped and murdered everywhere they went – only the children of devils could have done what they had done to people. I was happy to help them die for their emperor. I have seen some terrible, terrible things – things I have refused to speak about over the years because they were things which upset me too much; maybe now is the time to tell some of them.

I remember even before Arakan going on a patrol and finding a small village in the jungle. It was not unusual to find small settlements of people including native people who chose to live in the jungle as opposed to living in the towns and villages. The Japanese had been there and killed everyone in the village. Even the dogs had been slaughtered, but only their heads had been left behind by the Japanese, as they had taken the bodies with them for food. I remember there were a number of women and small children all dead; all the women had obviously been raped then bayoneted to death and their breasts cut off. The children had suffered the same fate: even the little girls had been raped by these beasts. We found several men of the village tied to trees covered in bayonet wounds and with their tongues cut out. Some had their penises sliced off and stuck in their mouths; others had their abdomens sliced open. I recall seeing a wild pig eating from the abdominal cavity of one of the dead men. For me, what was that like? I couldn't believe that any human being could do this to another. I remember how I felt physically ill at first, then I felt anger, such anger. These simple people had been living human beings a day or so ago and now they were dead; for what reason? The Japanese had killed them simply because they were there. A report was made about what we had found and then a burial party was organized to bury these unfortunate souls. We talked about it later as soldiers always do. One of my friends said to me, 'Jazzy [he always called me Jazzy not Jaspal], I swear I will where possible never take a Japanese alive, not after this.' I tried to reason with him, and I said to him, 'Not every Japanese is like that or would do what those Japanese did. We have to be careful not to become like them.' That's what I said to him as at that time. I felt maybe somehow our journey to heaven depended on how we behaved in this world. If we behaved as savages, God would not want us to share his realm. War changes men; men become different in war to how they are in peace. Was I myself overtly brutal during my war? Only God himself can judge my actions, taking into consideration the circumstances I and my fellow soldiers found ourselves in.

Former Lance-Corporal Andy Sloan was another Fourteenth Army veteran I had the pleasure of speaking with. Andy was a jovial, pleasant-natured old man who always had a smile on his face until the Japanese were mentioned. Then his whole persona would change, much like a light being switched off:

I was a kid really at the time; I was only 21 years old. I hadn't really been anywhere previous to the war and joining up with lots of my old schoolmates. The Fourteenth Army became a kind of surrogate family to me during my service, my duty to King, Country and Empire as they used to tout to us young lads. We felt we could do anything back then. Joining up was easy as long as you were found medically fit for the army. Report here to this depot, you'd have your hair cut right short, given your boots, uniform and kit and off you went to learn how to march and become a soldier of the British Army. The drill was intense and not everyone liked it; there was a lot of discipline and anyone who got out of line with the drill sergeant, then God help them. He was a right tough bastard that one: Mellings was his name and he was a typical sergeant – big with that bulldog's expression. I remember one day during rifle drill one lad lost his rag with this Sergeant Mellings, so Sergeant Mellings roared into his face, 'Anytime you believe you are man enough, lad, you just give me the word.' At that the lad quietened down. No, Mellings wasn't the sort of man you'd cross. He had a large scar across his face which he said he got in a brawl outside a bar in Edinburgh after a night's drinking there. The bloke he was fighting with pulled a knife on him, but he said he got the better of him. When I asked what happened, he just said, 'Well, lad, he's still alive. I can tell you that much.' Before we left for Burma he just pulled me and a few mates aside and told us, 'Look, the enemy you're going to fight out there isn't like those in Europe; you lads have pulled the shortest straw. Watch your fucking arses – the Japs kill without remorse; their mentality towards killing isn't like ours, so keep your wits about you at all times and never ever drop your guard for a minute.' I never forgot that all through the years.

Of course, when we got to Burma, we soon heard all the horror stories of what the Japs did in China at Nanking and some of the things that they'd done to those they had captured. It was vile things – really, totally inhumane. I honestly thought sometimes that it was all propaganda just so we would fight better as soldiers. Yet, one guy I became pals with over there had some photos of the work the Japs had been doing. The photos were horrific: one showed a woman who had been raped with a bayonet. Yes, one of the bastards had shoved a bayonet all the way inside her vagina; they had cut the fingers off small children, bayoneted babies, cut penises off the males, even tied some of their victims to ant mounds. It was all totally inhuman to me and yes, I saw these things with my own eyes later. Up until that point I was just a soldier of the Fourteenth doing my duty. After seeing these atrocities for myself I hated the Japs and actively sought to kill them. We of the Fourteenth Army bore the brunt of fighting the Japanese, they were a tough enemy and there were times when we thought we'd never get the true measure of them, yet hate is a funny thing, hate drives a man like no other emotion. Yes, I hated the

Japanese with a passion and yes, I collected a few gold teeth in the process, but I wasn't the only one who did that. Some of us would check the bodies of Japs we killed; we looked in their mouths and if there were gold teeth, we'd get them out using a bayonet – just gouge them out of their gums. The gold could be traded later and there were never any questions asked.

As the Fourteenth Army began working up towards operations, things were not always plain sailing, especially on the part of the Indian clerical establishment. Corps Headquarters had been neither mobile nor efficient, and training had to be carried out in order to make it both. All personnel, including staff officers, signallers, cooks, clerks and mess waiters were subjected to physical training. This would herald the start of each day, followed by route marches which were steadily increased in distance and toughness each day, accompanied by some brisk drill under selected instructors from the 70th Division. It was General Slim's opinion that in jungle warfare there was no such thing as a 'non-combatant': he had learned this through the retreat from Burma. Everyone had to undergo weapons training with qualification courses in rifle, pistol, Bren gun, bayonet, mortar and grenades. The idea that every man was trained to use every weapon available would later prove vital in the battles to come. The Indian HQ clerical establishment took an instant dislike to their enforced physical regimen and soon began to protest. The following grievances were conveyed to the British Commanding Officer General Slim:

(1) In many years of honourable service, we have never been subjected to such indignity as parades.
(2) The drill instructors are harsh men who often use bad language.
(3) The exhaustion consequent on these warlike goings-on render us incapable of performing our clerical duties.
(4) If compelled to continue this violent exercise, all the internal organs of our bodies – enumerating with unblushing detail – will cease to function and we will indubitably die.
(5) Our boots are wearing out.

In a scene reminiscent of a *Carry On* film, on the third morning of the new training regime and prior to a dreaded route march, a whole section of Indian clerks paraded sick. The variation in their medical complaints included aches, pains and general distresses. General Slim advised the doctor attending the men that, 'Whatever is or is not wrong with them now, I rely upon you to see that they really do feel ill within the next couple of hours.' What concoctions he may have administered to the clerks remains unknown, but pale and shaken they were on parade the next morning. General Slim made a point of asking the men, 'Are you in need of referral to the doctor again today?' To which every man replied that they were in no further need of any medical attention. Such lapses in discipline were not uncommon within any army, but nonetheless had to be dealt with most severely as a serious task lay ahead.

Slim recalled one humorous moment in his memoirs regarding his Gurkha orderly, a man named Bajbir, who protested when ordered to parade at the firing range. 'He said, "Who me?" and I replied to him, "Yes, you, you will go to the range to shoot at paper targets." Bajbir then protested, "But sir, I have killed five Japs!" All the same he paraded and proved himself an excellent shot at all positions and ranges. I am happy to say he later became an instructor.'

With HQ finally at a stage of mobility, fitness and readiness required for its future tasks there was now the subject of both the fear of the jungle and the 'Japanese bogey' which needed to be addressed. Slim drafted a memorandum consisting of tactical lessons learned during the 1942 defeat. The main points follow:

(1) The individual soldier must learn, by living, moving, and exercising in it that the jungle is neither impenetrable nor unfriendly. When he has once learned to move and live in it, he can master it for concealment, covered movement, and surprise attack upon the enemy.

(2) Patrolling is the master key to jungle fighting. All units, not only infantry battalions, must learn to patrol in the jungle, boldly, widely, cunningly, and offensively.

(3) All units must get used to having Japanese parties in their rear, and, when this happens, regard not themselves, but the Japanese as 'surrounded'.

(4) In defence, no attempt should be made to hold long, continuous lines. Avenues of approach must be covered and enemy

penetrations between our posts dealt with at once by mobile local reserves who have completely reconnoitred the country.

(5) There should rarely be frontal attacks and never frontal attacks on narrow fronts. Attacks should follow hooks and come in from flank or rear, while pressure holds the enemy in front.

(6) Tanks can be used in almost any country except swamp. In close country they must always have infantry with them to defend and reconnoitre for them. They should always be used in the maximum numbers available and capable of being deployed. The basic rule being 'the more you use, the fewer you lose'.

(7) There is no such thing as a non-combatant in jungle warfare. Every unit and sub-unit, including medical ones, is responsible for its own all-round protection, including patrolling, at all times.

(8) If the Japanese are allowed to hold the initiative, they are formidable. When we have it, they are confused and easy to kill. By mobility away from roads, surprise, and offensive action. we must regain and keep the initiative.

Slim purposely omitted the issue of air supply, as at the time he had no transport aircraft at his disposal. Should it become available then all well and good, but at that stage he decided that it was a good idea to not promise his men anything which he was not in a position to give them. Such unfulfilled promises had a bad effect on morale.

Living accommodation devised for the jungle camps was far from five star. Accommodation consisted of either tents or *bashas*, a simple hut which could easily be constructed from bamboo cane and finished with a thatching of leaves. These bashas were reasonably airy and cool but by no means waterproof in the wet season. Much could be learned from the native tribes who inhabited the jungle, especially the aboriginal tribes of the Ranchi plateau. Described as a friendly race of people with good physique, the men from these tribes constructed roads while their women provided most of the labour within the camps. The younger women wore nothing from above their waists. There were initial concerns about what effect this may have on the soldiers who worked among them in the camp. In all, however, the bare-breasted native girls, many of whom were very attractive indeed, proved unproblematic. Good conduct of the soldiers was maintained through strict army discipline.

Reginald Parry, who served in the Burma campaign, recalled the young native girls with some glee.

> When you've been away from home for such a long time and hardly seen a young woman, the sight of one with her assets on full display can have an embarrassing effect on a normal red-blooded male [he laughs]. It's a known fact all soldiers jerk off at night if away from home, wives and girlfriends – it's perfectly natural thing. Some of the lads copping an eyeful of a half-naked native girl found them too much, and they'd be wanking themselves off all bloody night and you'd have to shout at them, 'Look, for fuck's sake, will you stop fucking wanking? I'm trying to sleep here!' Some of the native girls were very pretty, but the chances of sneaking away with one of them for a bit of nookie in the jungle were very remote indeed. Though, no doubt it must have happened; some lad must have got lucky with one or two of them. If you got caught doing something like that though, the consequences could be very serious: you could be put on a charge of gross misconduct or worse. 'Stick to your hand and your imagination,' they used to say: 'That way you won't get the clap [VD] and you won't get into any trouble!' The soldier's philosophy – wonderful though isn't it [he laughs].

Another indomitable force in the forthcoming Burma campaign was that of United States Army General Joseph Warren Stillwell. Described as possessing a caustic personality, General Stillwell was nicknamed 'Vinegar Joe". Possessed of a brilliant military mind, Stillwell's distrust of the Allies and lack of resources meant that he was a man constantly forced to improvise. It was stated that Stillwell had been allocated one of the most difficult assignments of any theatre of war. For Stillwell the first step to fighting the war against the Japanese was the reformation of the Chinese Army. There were immense political issues to overcome, and the Chinese themselves were not overtly co-operative. The Indian government are also apprehensive of the possibility of having thousands of Chinese troops in their country. It was an admirable feat that Stillwell overcame all of the political, social and cultural difficulties in raising his large force of Chinese, who in the event would give a good account of themselves in the battles to come.

It is interesting to note at this point that neither the Japanese nor the Allied forces wished to fight a war in Burma. When the Japanese entered the war on the side of the Axis powers in December 1941, her main objective was to acquire raw materials, particularly oil, rubber and tin, through military expansion of what the Japanese termed the Greater Asian Co-Prosperity Sphere in order to create space for the Japanese population of the overcrowded home islands – similar to the Nazi intentions of occupying Soviet Russia for *Lebensraum*, or living space.

Another reason behind the Japanese invasion of Burma was that the Japanese knew it would be beneficial to them if they were able to cut off overland access to China from Burma via the famed Burma Road. The Burma Road was used to provide a steady stream of military aid from Rangoon, over the mountains and into Nationalist China. The Japanese knew, if this route was severed, they could then deprive the Chinese Nationalist armies of their lifeblood and ability to wage war, leaving Japan free to conquer the rest of China.

In addition, the possession of Burma would place the Japanese at the gates of India, where they believed general insurrection against the British Raj could be encouraged once Japanese troops had gained a foothold in Assam, a short distance from Calcutta. The Japanese cultivated the services of the dissident Bengal politician Chandra Bose, who recruited thousands of Indian troops captured at Singapore, convincing them to join his Indian National Army (INA) to fight against the British alongside the Japanese. There were many Indians who resented British rule of their country, as previously mentioned, but when statistics are compared it shows most Indians stood and fought valiantly alongside the British, ignoring the call of Chandra Bose to join his disloyal band, the INA.

Chapter 8

Welcome to the Jungle

One couldn't possibly write about the jungle war against the Japanese without any admirable mention of what became known as the Chindits. The Chindits, the brainchild of British Army officer Major-General Orde Charles Wingate, DSO, saw action in the jungles of Burma from 1943 to 1945. Officially conceived as the Long Range Penetration Groups, the Chindits, made up of large infantry elements of British Empire forces, were predominantly a special operations force and as each sub-unit within the Chindits had to be specially selected, they were rightly regarded as a special forces group. In fact, the Chindits were the largest Allied special forces group of the Second World War. On paper this may all sound very glamourous, yet it has to be said that anyone entering the ranks of the Chindits understood they were undertaking what was in effect 'a serious gamble with their own life'. Being a Chindit was without doubt one of the most dangerous occupations of the war. Training was exceptionally tough, and the unit spent months in India prior to the commencement of operations learning how to live, move and fight in the jungle without regular lines of supply or infrastructure around them. Their primary role was to travel on foot deep into the jungle behind enemy lines where they would endeavour to disrupt Japanese operations, wreak havoc and kill as many Japanese as possible. Their missions included the destruction of railway lines, bridges and enemy logistical hubs, and to harass the Japanese, thus forcing them to commit resources from other fronts. It is a sobering fact that many soldiers who entered the jungle as Chindits did not return – they were either killed, wounded or fell ill due to jungle conditions, conditions such as malaria and dysentery. An equal number became separated during jungle firefights only to become lost and never seen again. However, the Japanese soon learned to both fear and respect these remarkable soldiers.

The first Chindit foray into Japanese territory was by the 77th Indian Infantry Brigade who marched into occupied Burma in 1943 under Operation Longcloth that saw 3,000 men marching over a thousand miles during the campaign. The second operation, on a much larger scale, was called Operation Thursday and took place in March 1944 and consisted of a force of 20,000 men. It was also the second-largest airborne operation of the Second World War. Air support for the operation was provided by the 1st Air Commando USAAF. Sadly, General Wingate was killed a few weeks after the launch of this operation.

The Chindits were typically comprised of multiple infantry regiments, a commando company, eight sections of the Royal Air Force, a signal section, and a mule transport company. Food, weapons, water, ammunition and everything else required for their operations had to be carried by themselves. Each Chindit soldier had to carry more than seventy-two pounds of equipment, proportionately more than the mules requisitioned to carry the support weapons and other supplies. Typically, a Chindit had to carry his standard weapon, either a .303 Lee Enfield rifle or 9mm Sten sub-machine gun, ammunition, grenades, a machete or Gurkha kukri knife, seven days' worth of rations, groundsheet, change of uniform along with other miscellaneous items of kit. This was all carried in an Everest carrier, essentially a metal rucksack frame without the pack. When supplies ran short the Chindits relied entirely on airdrops for resupply, although these were not always forthcoming when required due to the nature of warfare. The Chindits' first expedition against the Japanese forces did not see any direct combat with the enemy but damaged critical enemy infrastructure. This came as a shock to the Japanese on the receiving end and forced Japanese commanders to put their forces on the offensive, allocating troops to attacks upon Allied forces which not only sacrificed valuable military resources but also manpower. On the part of the Chindits, their endeavours, although successful, were highly costly: a third of Chindit troops were lost. One of the grimmest aspects of being a Chindit was facing the reality that if you as an individual became too ill or weak to keep up with the other men of your unit, you would be left behind, basically abandoned to your fate.

Former Chindit Gilbert Summers was a man I had known for many years living in the same Cotswold village of Broadway in Worcestershire. He lived along the Cheltenham Road where I once lived, and we regularly shared lifts to work as we both worked at the same local food production factory in the nearby town of Evesham. Gilbert was a man who did not readily discuss his military service, yet if you asked him, he was always happy to tell you stories. As a young man I had still to realize the value the stories from our war veterans and I wish I had recorded more when I had the chance. Having learned that Gilbert had been a Chindit, which I admit I knew very little about back then, I asked him what the worst thing about being a Chindit was. He responded:

> Well, if you became sick, which a lot of men did due to the diseases and infections which were rife in the jungles of Burma and the Far East, you'd had it. The same applied to any men who had been wounded in any way. These men – and while I say men, many would in some cases be your best mates – if they could not keep up with the patrol which had to keep moving for obvious reasons then they would have to be left behind. There was no way incapacitated men could be catered for in Chindit operations: we had to keep moving, doing our job and moving on. I knew one man personally whom we had to leave behind because he had a wound in his leg which became worse to the point where he couldn't walk let alone march. The wound became badly infected and caused fever among other things. We said our last words to him as a friend, gave him some cigarettes and shook his hand and then we had to move on and leave him behind in that jungle. I heard a report a while later from a small patrol that passed by the spot where we left him. I think they were Indians. They found blood and drag marks; they said it wasn't the Japanese that got him but probably a tiger or another big cat – they couldn't find any remains. It was pretty upsetting at the time. Lots of good men went that same way, left behind to die, discovered by wild animals or found by the Japanese and tortured to death.

On the subject of killing the Japanese, I asked Gilbert if he had personally killed any Japanese soldiers, to which he replied, 'Unfortunately, yes, I killed one with my knife once. It was not pleasant, killing a man, never is, but it was a duty, our job to do so.'

102

I recall after work the one day going back to Gilbert's house. After putting his ferocious German shepherd out into the back garden, he came back with a commando-style fighting knife. He warned me before taking the knife out of its sheath, 'Watch this, lad – it's razor sharp.' I drew the knife from its sheath and marvelled at the piece of history I was holding in my hand. I asked Gilbert, 'Is this the knife you used to kill the Japanese by any chance?' To which he replied, 'Yes, it is.' There was no bravado with this man whatsoever: he spoke quietly, wearing the stern expression he always wore when discussing anything to do with war. Again, I bitterly regret not learning the whole of Gilbert's story. He now lies at rest in the Catholic cemetery along the Leamington Road in Broadway. His grave, which I visited in 2015, bears the familiar dates of birth and death as well as the inscription, 'Gilbert Summers – 'CHINDIT'. I stood before the grave for a few minutes and, as I reflected, I saw his face and heard his voice again, recalling the chicken sheds he once had along the Childswickham Road from where he once sold fruit and vegetables. I later walked down that same road to see if the sheds were still there. They were long gone – even the driveway leading into them was now a hedge and the ground where his sheds once stood a ploughed field. It was like he had never existed: as with many the graves are all that's left of these remarkable characters.

As the Chindits were getting to grips with their Japanese enemy via infiltration behind enemy lines, so the men of the Fourteenth Army were learning to do the same. Mark Rutherford recalled:

> Those first steps into those jungles in Burma were like us landing on the moon. We'd received our training and were reasonably acclimatized to the region, but it was still bloody hard slog all the way. Everything about going into the jungle was a hard slog; it was a demanding and dangerous environment without there being Japs in there. I remember when we first began to push into the jungle, you'd get these apes high up in the jungle canopy where they surveyed the territory all around them. Once these fucking things were alerted to your presence, you would be greeted by a crescendo of shrieks, hoots and howls. I remember Sergeant Johns had to stop one of the lads who was aiming his .303 up at one of these apes and was about to shoot it.

When old Johnsie, as we called him, challenged the lad, he stood there shaking with that all-too-familiar look of terror in his eyes and he said, 'They will give our position away to the fucking Japs.' So old Johnsie, bless him, said to the lad. 'Look, the fucking Japs already know we're here lad.' There were a few stifled laughs, I can tell you, but it wasn't funny really, as the Japs knew we were coming and were preparing a welcome party for us. When it kicked off, it wasn't so much a battle; it was just a quick skirmish to let us know that they were there, I guess.

It was about a couple of days in I reckon. We'd spent the night from hell in that jungle and few of us could sleep due to the unfamiliarity of the place. It was pitch black and you'd hear all these strange noises and you'd think, 'What the fuck is that? Is it a Jap or an animal?' You just didn't know and your nerves were constantly shot. The ground seemed alive with every variety of pestilence. Things crawled on you in the dark and mosquitoes buzzed around your face and ears. Even in the daytime you were constantly on edge all the time and you dared not relax. We heard stories of Japs sneaking up on an unsuspecting Brit and cutting his throat before his mates even knew what was going on. A lot of it was bollocks but was designed to make you keep your wits about you. At night we slept hugging our rifles; you never let your rifle go and you kept it in your hands at the ready just in case.

I recall one dawn – it must have been a Jap patrol; they were not really quiet or sneaky as we heard them coming through the bushes. The next thing all hell breaks loose, the .303 Bren gun opens up on them and I see this feller with a tin helmet with camouflage on its top go flying backwards. The burst from the Bren literally picked him up and threw him backwards through the air; I remember seeing the soles of his boots and thinking, 'Fucking hell, look at that!' I saw Gurkha Jaspal Gahor draw his kukri and rush forward into the trees in front of us shouting, '*Ayo Gorkhali*' ['The Gurkhas are upon you!'] as he went. It was like something out of a fucking John Wayne movie;

it was like unreal. I hadn't seen him but Jaspal had noticed a Jap lying on the ground fumbling with something. Anyway, he rushes forward and there's all this shouting and thrashing around of the trees and stuff, followed by more rifle shots then the noise steadily subsides. Jaspal comes back with a pair of lugholes [ears] in his hand. I say to him, 'What the fuck have you got there?' and he's proudly holding up these fucking Jap lug holes. The Japs had fled back into the jungle; the Bren really saved our necks on this occasion. The lads were alert and ready and had opened up on them as soon as they came into view despite their heavy camouflage. One of the Japs had rushed forward with a grenade in his hands; he was brought down by a rifle shot but he was still alive – this is the Jap Gurkha Jaspal went after; he said he could see him trying to pull the pin out of the grenade and stopped him. I asked him how he did it and he told me he cut the Jap's head off with one blow. Then he cut the ears off to prove that he'd killed one of them. Afterwards, I said to him, 'What you going to do with those lugholes – put them in tonight's curry or something?' We had a laugh about it. Then we had to get going before the Japs sent a bigger force out to have a go at us as we were sure they would do. We reported back about what happened and the position on the map etc. We took no dead or wounded in that action but had killed at least four Japanese soldiers in their patrol. We don't know for sure how many of them there were, but we got the better of them. I remember looking at the Jap bodies – the first Japanese soldiers I ever saw were these dead ones. One of the lads was busy cutting pieces of uniform off the one body. He wanted souvenirs and checked the dead Japs pockets and everything. Then Johnsie comes striding over and tells him to put it all back. Johnsie was a funny bloke like that – he didn't think it was right taking things off dead bodies. This made him an unpopular figure at times among the other men, but I liked him.

The idea was then to keep going, make contact with the enemy by setting up ambush points along the way in the jungle. We had these .303 Vickers heavy machine guns,

First World War technology but deadly effective as long as you kept them cool. When you set up a camp for the night, you had to devise a secure perimeter defended by the Vickers, two-inch-calibre mortars and Bren guns and then a series of watchmen whose job it was to alert the camp of any Jap intrusions. Your ears soon became tuned to what were normal sounds in the jungle at night. You learned from experience certain sounds of an incoming Jap attack. They were not always as stealthy as they probably hoped to be. Typical signs of the Japs coming were noises of startled jungle birds and animals. No matter how hard you try to approach silently, you're going to make some noise as you move through dense foliage. It was just these little things you had to remember and of course to alert the camp an attack was coming.

I did watch duty many times. Your eyes never really became acclimatized to jungle darkness as it was pitch black to the point that your eyes often played tricks on you. If you stared hard enough for long enough into pitch darkness, you began seeing things that weren't there, like strange purple colours and things. You asked yourself, 'Is it my imagination?' I tell you it's fucking scary shit, it really is; it fucks with your mind and anyone who has been there and done it – fucking respect to them. I can see why some blokes lost it in the jungle and I sympathized greatly with them. Most of the time you only slept when you became totally knackered, so tired you couldn't stay awake if you tried. It was all too easy in the darkness of the jungle to open fire on anything that moved. too. If you weren't on watch and you managed to sleep, when you woke up, you would be covered in insect bites. I remember squeezing pus out of infected bites; you see, they didn't dry up and scab over like in a normal climate. In the heat and constant damp of the jungle wounds often turned messy and became infected as a matter of course. These bug things even got into your rations, and you could see them floating in the greasy residue – it was fucking horrible and I hated it. I just wanted the war to hurry up and end so we could go back home, but the hard slog still lay ahead. We all knew that this was just the start of our war here in Burma.

Ron Rastall recalled one of his first experiences of moving into the jungle to take the fight to the Japanese.

They put me on night watch duty, and I was one of a few fellers tasked with this night watch-cum-guard duty. You had an area in front of you to watch and you had your rifle and grenades at the ready just in case. Problem at night was you could see fuck all; it was pitch black in there, a Jap could have crawled right up, and you'd never know he was there. After some minutes your eyes acclimatized to the darkness to a degree, yet there were things in the jungle other than Japs, all kinds of animals, some dangerous some not dangerous. I don't know what exactly happened this one night, but one lad fired his 9mm Sten sub-machine gun at something which was moving along the ground towards him. Pretty soon others began firing and all hell broke out until the order to cease firing was given. It was determined that the lad had seen nothing and that his eyes were playing tricks on him, though he later told me personally that what he had fired on was really weird as the bullets of the Sten gun were bouncing off whatever it was. He had no explanation for it at all, but I knew the lad well and knew he wasn't one for telling tales and stuff. We never did find out what it was he had fired on and it was no good asking the natives as they would tell you it was some devil of the jungle or something as natives are a superstitious lot, aren't they?

Learning to stay calm, cool and collected at night in the jungle took a hell of a lot of discipline. It was a very frightening place to have to be in and any man who says he wasn't scared was a fucking liar, because I was shit scared most of the time. I got friendly with a Gurkha sergeant; he was great that man was, and I always felt relatively safe with him around. He could distinguish natural sounds of the jungle from unnatural man-made sounds; even at night he knew whether to relax or be ready for trouble.

The Gurkhas possessed some great natural ability and skills in the jungle. If they felt as shit scared as what I did, then they certainly hid it well and never showed they were scared. They were great to have around, especially when a firefight broke out: they just wanted to get in there with those fucking knives. I saw them carve Japs up to death with them. They were some of the best soldiers in the Fourteenth.

Tommie Watkins recalls his baptism of fire in the jungle:

I remember as we marched off and the noise of civilization being replaced by that of some other alien world. We crossed a small river, around waist deep, nothing too bad. We climbed the bank the other side and immediately saw that leeches had attached themselves to our legs. One lad had a petrol lighter and used that to try and burn the leeches so they'd loosen their grip; he ended up burning his leg in the process [he laughs], daft sod. The idea was to burn them so they let go; if you just pulled them off there was the danger of infection as the jaws could be left behind in your skin. Leeches, however unpleasant, were the least of our worries. The first man we lost in our section was killed in a fall. We were working our way up through a series of large rocks beside a waterfall. All I recall hearing is an ear-piercing scream as the man fell. You couldn't see the bottom of the waterfall as there was too much foliage covering it. Two men volunteered to go back down to aid the fallen man, but they could find no sign of him and he must have drowned and been swept away by the vicious current. The decision to push on was made and on we went. After that I recall thinking, 'That could easily have been you, Tommie boy.'

As we pushed deeper into the Burmese jungle, we saw all kinds of weird things. I once saw a spider sitting on a large leaf, the thing had a leg span as wide as my hand; it just gave me the creeps looking at it. We had some Burmese guides along with us and they thought we were hilarious that we were scared of these things. To them all of this was like us going for a walk in the park back home. At a certain point the soldiers who smoked were told they couldn't smoke. There was uproar at this order, but good reason for it being given. In the jungle cigarette smoke hangs in the humid air for hours and it indicates to your enemy that you have passed by. It can leave a scent trail direct to your camp, so smoking was prohibited

We learned the Japs were nearby and that we would be reinforced for an attack on their position. We were told to stop and discard all heavy kit which would be left at camp and we were to take only weapons, ammunition and full canteens of water, nothing else. We had to leave all personal belongings behind in our kitbags, including letters, cigarette cases, pipes, anything of value really, apart from wedding rings. This is when the heart begins to pound, the mouth goes dry and you begin to feel physically sick. You know you are going into a fight; you worry about getting lost or separated, wounded or killed. You just think, this is it, this is the time that decides whether or not I am a good soldier as I have been trained to be – or a coward, the stigma of which I couldn't live with. You have all these emotions pulling your mind in different directions, then the order to move out is given. You snake your way as stealthily as you can through the entangled foliage, bushes, streams, rivers and trees, your weapon at the ready. The Japs had made a clearing; in fact it was a few huts that the natives had obviously abandoned. We crept around their flanks and observed them for some minutes, trying to ascertain how many were there. We counted at least one Type 99 machine gun with crew sitting next to the weapon. The idea was to take these little bastards out first and then mop up the rest. They seemed surprisingly non-vigilant considering they knew we must have been nearby in the area, but we had hoped our stealthy approach would pay off.

It was an Indian corporal who initiated the attack. There was a succession of loud cracks; I saw the three Japs by the Type 99 fall back dead, shot through the head. The whole patrol opened up as the Japs tried to find cover. One of them dived beneath one of the huts, Private Collinson opened fire with the Bren which soon brought the whole structure crashing down on the Jap. The Bren was cutting branches of nearby trees and leaves, and pieces of wood and shit was flying all over the place. We all poured rounds into them and there was some return fire, but it appeared wild and uncoordinated. It seemed to happen every attack we carried out: you'd get one or two diehard Japs come rushing out from nowhere with a sword raised above their heads. These Japs were shot down in an instant before they could inflict any savagery. Their swords were later picked up and these were allowed to be kept as souvenirs. Grenades were thrown in, then a cease fire was ordered. It went deathly silent as we waited for some minutes; we had them surrounded so there was no way out for them. We had hoped to capture some of the Japs alive but as we slowly moved forward like a cat might stalk a bird, it became apparent that we had killed them all. Even the one buried under the collapsed hut was dead. Their camp was searched for any intelligence material and a map was discovered. It was taken for our intelligence guys to examine and it turned up a few interesting points for us. You had to be careful though as the map could have been deliberately left there as some kind of feint or trap. We collected up the Jap weapons and looked around, picking up a few Jap flags as we then moved back to our camp.

That night we had more sentries posted on watch than the previous nights. It was a good job as at around 3.30 a.m. our camp came under sustained attack. Again, the Bren guns proved most valuable in repelling a force of some thirty Japs. I remember a flare going up and seeing a Jap wriggling around, entangled in some barbed wire we had strung around the camp perimeter. I put three shots into him, and he moved no more. What shocked me was their suicidal nature of attack – they would just rush forward full on into the rifle and machine-gun fire; it wasn't bravery in my book, it was madness. They'd rush forward hurling grenades with their meatball flags hanging from their rifles and screaming, bayoneting anything in their path.

We lost people in this one and it was a sobering experience. Most of our dead had been caught outside the perimeter and had been stabbed multiple times with bayonets. That was the thing with the Japs I just didn't get: they'd rather kill you with a bayonet than with a bullet. They wanted you to die with a savagery in fitting with their own warped mentality. They wanted you to feel the death they were dealing you, for you to die in agony. Once you have witnessed this, you felt it is less of an issue to take any of them prisoner. I later shot Japs who tried to surrender to me; if there was no one around who could later hold me to account, I killed them there and then, armed or not, wounded or dying.

Later on, I was talking to one of the Indians who found himself outside of the wire. He told me:

'They [the Japanese] were running all around me. I was lying beneath some jungle plants and they ran straight past me without seeing me lying there.' He then smiled very broadly and said, 'You see, jungle is good, jungle is friend always.' I liked the Indians and I have still yet to meet one who can't turn the most revolting thing into a culinary delight. Despite the daily struggles and the horrors, the Indians proved a morale booster. They were always friendly and jovial and could turn even a monkey's corpse into a curry fit for a king. Yes, we had snake, rat, wild pig, even jungle birds that the Indians could then whip up into something to augment our ration supplies. They also made very good sentries as they, like the Gurkhas, had a fine ear tuned to the environment and were able to distinguish natural sounds from those which were unnatural or manmade. They could judge distance and direction and speed of anything moving in the dark. Often, we heard things crashing around and we'd grab our weapons just for one of the Indians to calmly announce, 'It's just a pig, over there, about a hundred yards away.'

Akihara Koto recalled that the Japanese were just as spooked in the jungle as their western enemy:

We would hear things when darkness fell, not that the jungle offers much light to those who choose to inhabit it.

111

Often rotten trees would creak, followed by a loud snap and then the tree would come crashing down. Treefalls occurred frequently in the jungles of Asia; when you heard a tree falling you hoped it did not fall upon you and your friends. Night-time and dawn were always the best times in which to mount an attack upon your foe. I feel that we as Japanese soldiers fought well all times of the day. If you are resigned to only operating at certain times of the day, then your tactical efficiency diminishes, and you become ineffective while your enemy gains strength over you. Some of the first combats I took part in were testing the enemy's spearpoint, seeing how their frontal probing forces reacted. Our idea in meeting them was simple: we would camouflage ourselves very heavily so if we remained still, we would remain unseen; the idea was to become a part of the jungle until the enemy was very close. Ambush is a very easy principle, yet we could not afford to simply lie in wait and ambush the enemy – we had to go on the attack too. In our attacks we tried to overwhelm the enemy by firing our weapons and throwing grenades into them from their flanks. Those that fell did so in the divine service of the Emperor; there could be no greater honour at that time. Yes, it is true those of us who carried a sword would draw our swords as we moved forward. It was considered an honour to kill with the sword as, to the Japanese, the sword possessed great spiritual significance. You say about killing with bayonets, that maybe this is barbaric. Bayonets were made for the purpose of killing at close range. What difference is there? Killing is killing, is it not? We were well rehearsed in using the bayonet as a weapon. It of course required great courage to charge forward with the intent of not only shooting enemy soldiers but stabbing them too. We used every weapon at our disposal and there was little time to argue the merits of each weapon and their ethical uses; this at that time was not a consideration in our thinking. To destroy the enemy was the sole concept. In many aspects the jungle offered a neutral environment in which to fight a battle; only those who understood the jungle, could master its complexities and master the art of living within it and killing the enemy who also lived within it. Soon full-scale battles involving many men would take place; we knew that, and we felt confident all the time – we had come far, we had learned much and it was our belief that we could not lose. Our ruthlessness, as it is termed today, in my opinion was not being brutal – it symbolized our confidence.

If the initial skirmishes with the Japanese were anything to go by, it reinforced to the men of the Fourteenth Army that they were facing an enemy who would not give up easily, who was prepared to take casualties in order to inflict losses upon his western enemies. As the jungle became the battleground every bit as unforgiving as the enemy they faced, the men of the Fourteenth Army soon learned that the jungle with its many varied characteristics had its advantages. They were determined that if the jungle was to be a hell for them, then they would in turn make it a greater hell for their Japanese adversary.

Chapter 9

Letters Home

From a morale point of view a simple letter from home was essential for any soldier engaged in active service sometimes thousands of miles away from home. Ever since soldiers first set out on campaigns around the world, the need for communication with their family and loved ones back home was of vital importance, not only for morale but also their psychological wellbeing. However, it was soon learned that a degree of control had to be exercised over the content of letters written by soldiers to their families, applying in particular to those involved in the conflicts throughout the twentieth century. Prior to censorship, a soldier could write practically anything he wished in a letter home. It was soon realized that censorship of contents was an essential component to the security of one's own operations. Should uncensored mail fall into the hands of your enemy, he might glean all manner of information on operational matters along with your state of morale. In the Far East during the Second World War, as with any other theatre of operations, the one thing a soldier looked forward to more than anything else was that letter from home.

Akihara Koto recalls:

> Hearing from our families was of vital importance to us. Often, we also received special bags with sake and other small treats from our families back home. They would send us news on what was going on at home. Of course, they were instructed to never mention anything bad to us, anything which might have an effect on our focus on things, so there were dos and don'ts for writing letters to those of us at war. While I was in the jungle, I received several letters all at once; there had been a delay in the mail getting through to our units, so they were weeks late

in arriving. My mother and father wrote to me with some wonderful news: my sister had given birth to her first child, a little girl. I was an uncle for the first time in my life and I felt honoured. I quickly told my friends within my unit and we all celebrated this wonderful occasion. However, I did think that I might not return home to see the baby, I could be killed or give my life accordingly. I wanted the child to know how proud I was and what I was doing just in case I did not come home to my family. There was no way I could have written things down in a letter that I wanted to say as it would have been an infringement of our military law. If such a letter fell into the hands of the enemy, their intelligence people would read it and use the information against us. So, you see, I couldn't write anything about where I was, what I had done or where we would be going next, not that I always knew. Our letters were therefore very bland and dull in their content because there was not much we could say apart from how bad or good the weather was, what the people were like here, the wildlife and flowers – things like that. I used to say I was very happy and in the best of health and then ask questions about family members back home. It must have been worse for my family back home having to read such dull writing; they could learn nothing from what I was saying other than I was alive – maybe for them that was enough.

Mark Rutherford also recalls the joy when the mail drop had been announced:

Fucking hell – letters! Who writes or reads letters these days; it's a forgotten art now, what with computers and things. For us letters were like gold back then; we always looked forward to a letter from home. My mom and dad wrote to me twice a week, sometimes more than that. Problem was if there was a hold-up along the route then it could take weeks for a letter to arrive with us. Sometimes I'd get a bundle of letters dating from weeks ago. I would arrange them in date order and go through them then make a note of any points I could address and then I'd write back and reply. The biggest problem of all was you couldn't say fuck all, for fear of giving away anything to the Japs if they were to intercept our mail. We would sit down and spend ages writing letters; once written, it wasn't a case of just sending them for posting with the regiment's other mail – it all had to be checked and stamped by the official censor. If a letter was cleared, then it would have an ink stamp stating it had been passed by the censor. Generally, we knew what we could and could not write in our letters, so in effect we were our own censors. We would have never included anything which might endanger the lives of either our unit or another. Most of my letters were just things saying I am fine, the weather's a bit shit, etc. etc. – nothing to rave about at all. Yes, it was frustrating as my old mom and dad had no idea what I had been involved in, that I'd been busy trying to kill Japs and things, and just trying to stay alive and that at times I wish I was back home instead of here. They only really understood what I'd been doing once I'd got back home and sat them down and told them everything. They were very shocked, and it scared them, so you can see if they'd have read the truth of what was really going on at the time, they would have both had heart attacks from the worry. In that way censorship was probably the best thing – what my mom and dad back home didn't know wouldn't cause them any worry.

Tommie Watkins enjoyed his deluge of mail from his mother and father and his sweetheart back home in England. He recalls:

I used to get loads of mail. My parents wrote me something every other day and my girlfriend Celine did too. The other blokes used to say to me, 'Fuck me Tommie, you got the whole of blighty writing to you or something?' If we had any delays in mail getting through to the front, it would pile up and I'd get even more [he laughs]. My mother and father just wrote things about their house and their garden and so and so sends you their best wishes, and I'd have best wishes from aunts and uncles and things like that. Obviously, the letters I wrote to Celine were ones where I professed my undying love for her [he laughs]. Oh, she was a beauty and I was very lucky that she was prepared to wait for me; she could have had her pick of any of the boys back home. I told her before I left for the Far East, 'When I get back, I want to marry you.' I'd tell her about how beautiful Asia was as a country, how diverse its people were, the wonderful clothes they wore, their religious practices and their hospitality, all that kind of thing mostly. I never once mentioned the Japs, how they attacked us and we them, and how many men we lost and how many they must have lost. It just wasn't the done thing; it wouldn't have been appropriate anyway I don't think. Everything we wrote got read and got checked by the censor. Not everyone was happy about this, I recall one of the lads saying, 'Fucking censor, nosy fucking parker more like.' No, I loved my letters and I loved writing something back; even if it wasn't that much it let the folks and Celine know I was alive and kicking and that I was okay.

Zero fighter pilot Hikokuru Ishimaru said of his letters to and from his home in Japan:

I wrote so as my family knew my morale was always high. I used a code word for if things were not good or if they were very good, so as my family would know what I was really feeling. In the early days we had no real worthy opponents in the air, so everything was going our way and my letters to my mother, father, brother and sister were always full of exuberance. I would tell them I was happy. If things were not good I would add the code word that only me and my family would be aware of; to anyone else reading my letter it would appear normal. I did push to see how much I could get away with, but it was never operational information – only things that had taken place weeks previous, so it would have been no use to an enemy intelligence officer. I did regularly have my photograph taken with my aircraft and would send a photo back home in my letters. My family loved seeing the photos I sent them: it made them happy and they would send photos to me, some of which I kept inside my aircraft as good luck charms.

Some of the letters from home, while moderate in their content, contained some pretty provocative enclosures as Mark Rutherford explains:

There was this young private soldier with us; he had this girlfriend back home who would put saucy photos inside his letters. He used to squeal with delight when his letters arrived, hoping there would be a photo inside. The thing was this young lady started to send photos of herself with barely anything on; they were pretty hot, and he would wave them in the air and show all the lads. It seemed that she became more daring with each photo she sent. I think they drew the line when she sent one which showed her lying on her back naked [he laughs]; that one I think he told me got confiscated. He told me that the CO took him aside and said to him, 'We have plenty of magazines with scantily clad young ladies here for your perusal, so there is little requirement for this X-certification to be sent to you through the mail.' He was pretty hurt over it but rules were rules – anything they felt was breaking the rules or went too far was taken away. The young lady in question was warned that her enclosures might have a detrimental effect upon a young man away on active service, so after that the saucy photos were no more. It wasn't really anything to hoot about, just the brass didn't like it very much as they felt even a photograph could prove a distraction. It was quite amusing really as I remember that lad. He said, 'Look Mark, when I get home after this bloody war has ended, I'm going to fuck the shit out of that girl and then I'm going to ask her to marry me.' I said to him, 'I'm sure her folks are going to say you got that the wrong way around, mate.' He did make it through the war and, fair enough to the lad, he did fuck the shit out of her and married her as I was invited along to the wedding [he laughs]. So, there you are, our letters weren't exciting at all apart from the odd photo that got through that probably shouldn't have. We used to say, 'What would a fucking Jap do with a photo of a naked girl, anyway? Maybe wank themselves silly over it.'

Ken Shaw was a Yorkshire man who hailed from the village of Cottingley near Bingley. Ken served with 355 Wireless Unit (WU) of the Royal Air Force. He had left the UK for the Far East in January 1943 and recalled:

355 WU was an intelligence-gathering unit. We had been specifically trained in intercepting and deciphering Japanese military radio traffic. This, although a pretty elite kind of task, meant I had virtually nothing I could tell my parents back home at Cottingley about what I was doing. As far as they knew I was going to the Far East with the British Royal Air Force and that was it – they knew nothing more. We left England in the January of 1943 and we headed to Cape Town in southern Africa; this was our halfway stop and we were there for a couple of months. I didn't write the first letter home to my parents until we docked at Calcutta in India. I wrote and told my folks about what colourful clothes the locals wore here in India. Now, I only fell foul of the military censors on one occasion and that was when I wrote how some of the British lads nicknamed the natives 'nig-nogs'. When my folks received this letter that word had been scrubbed out with black ink, but if you held the letter up to the light you could still read what I had written. Back then it wasn't such a big deal as it would be today, yet the censor still scrubbed it out, but it was the only time that ever happened to me. As I said, my line of work was so secret my folks could not be told anything at all about what I was doing and my exact location in India. I just used to tell them about the natives, the jungle environment, the flowers, the food, creepy crawlies and the rain, things like that really. My letters were dull and boring in many respects. I myself didn't realize just what a critical role we were to play in defeating the Japanese.

119

One of our main tasks was listening in on Japanese military radio transmissions in the Kohima and Imphal regions of north-east India, this just prior to when the Japanese laid siege to these two towns. In all I wrote over two hundred letters to my mother and father and yet not one of them gave the slightest hint of what I'd been doing out there. I always looked forward to hearing from mum and dad, bless them. They would tell me about the family, any new births, which flowers were now growing in the garden and how the weather was. It was just small talk really as we knew we could speak about little else or the letters would be rejected. We had very strict censorship, though the first line of censorship lay with us as the authors of our letters; it was up to us to make sure we didn't write anything we shouldn't and we didn't, as that was the rule. It was only when I got back home after the war that I was able to tell mum and dad about it all, how bad it had been and what a vulgar, terrible enemy we had faced out there. I still have all the letters I sent to my mother and father and also the ones they sent to me. When I read through them today, I think, 'What a load of rubbish!' – just boring, nothing of interest at all, but back then at that time these pieces of paper meant a hell of a lot to people. That's what one should remember with these things. I remember one fellow in my unit he used to fill his letter cards as they were known with poetry. He had a girlfriend back home in Yorkshire, and after writing that he was okay and wish you were here and all that stuff [he laughs], he would then write these poems to her. Some of them were pretty good, bit too slushy for some of the lads but they were good. He would sit there composing for bloody ages, crossing bits out and then adding others, then he would say to me, 'Hey, Kenny, what do you think to this? Do you reckon she will like it?' I'd say back to him, 'Go on then Shakespeare, let's have a listen.' Yes, so letters to and from home were important towards the war effort in many ways and helped keep long-distance love alive too.

I felt gravely sorry for some of the lads though. There was one I knew, the product of a troubled childhood, and had spent most of his life in a kind of kids' home, not very nice at all. He never used to get any letters at all, and I really felt for him; it was bloody sad. Me and some other lads got together and tried to find a way of sorting this out, so one of the lads suggested we set up a penfriend thing for those lads who didn't have any family and any mail. It turned out to be something of a success and pretty soon we had a load of letters come in, especially for those boys who didn't get anything. They would look at the addresses and see if any of the girls lived nearby to where they were from and they'd take it from there. Then they could send photos and write to each other and it cheered up the lads who had no family and boosted their morale. The lad I had always felt a bit sorry for did okay for himself when he got back home; that girl he had spent the next two years writing to wanted to get married. It was very nice, and I was happy for him. In fact, he came up to me and said, 'Ken, if it weren't for you, I wouldn't have ever met Lizzie. I would just like to thank you for that and when we tie the knot, would you please be my best man as I don't know anyone else that I would like to do it.' I felt really honoured and I told him, 'Sure, I would be delighted to be your best man.' So, you see, letters from home were essential to the war effort, and no doubt they were to the Japs too. We couldn't have got by without our mail; there was always a stink if the mail was late [he laughs].

Chapter 10

The Second Battle of Arakan

This chapter provides a brief insight into some aspects of the Second Battle of Arakan. Space constraints do not permit any extensive analysis. The second Battle of Arakan refers to that fought between the forces of the Japanese Empire and the British Fourteenth Army in Burma from 30 December 1943 to 6 April 1944. The bulk of the fighting fell to the Anglo-Indian XV Corps which was under the command of Lieutenant-General Philip Christison. XV Corps began its offensive at the Mayu Penninsula which lies in the Arakan region of Burma. Facing the soldiers of XV Corps was the Japanese 55th Division, under the command of Lieutenant General Hanaya Tadashi. Tadashi met the threat from the British XV Corps by dispatching units of the Sakurai Force of the Japanese 55th Division – Major General Sakurai Tokutaró – in small groups on 5 February. It was clear to the British that the Japanese could only be thwarted for a short period. There was also no clear intelligence as to enemy strength. The British, well versed in the strategy of their enemy, knew that any attack would arrive in the form of an outflanking manoeuvre, a tactic which had served the Japanese well in the past. In the event the small groups of the Sakurai Force were successful in penetrating the Indian 7th Division without being compromised. On the following day, the Japanese crossed the Kalapanzin River, attacking the forward headquarters of the Indian 7th Division, taking them completely by surprise. One of the Indians of the 7th Division recalled:

> Most important were the radios and communications equipment which we were told must not fall into the hands of the enemy. It was impossible to retreat at speed and have to try and move all of this equipment, so it was destroyed in situ before the Japanese took the position. We smashed the

radio sets with our rifle butts and cut all of the connecting leads and wires into as many pieces as we could, and we then burned it. It was imperative that none of this equipment fell into the hands of the enemy. Any paperwork not of importance to us was burned rather than being left intact.

General Slim ascertained that the Japanese were making their move when, upon leaving Lieutenant-General Sir Frank Messervy's headquarters and driving through the Ngakyedauk Pass while en route to the nearby airstrip, he noted the arrival of Japanese fighters in large numbers overhead. He noted: 'There were at least a hundred or more Japanese fighters in the sky above. Clearly this was a direct challenge to our air force and was the opening move of the Japanese attack.'

Unlucky for the Japanese, the RAF had the Supermarine Spitfire fighter aircraft at its disposal in theatre. It is true that the Japanese Zero fighters far outnumbered the Spitfires, yet the Spitfire was a superior fighter to the Zero which was now beginning to feel its age. Far from being intimidated, the pilots of the RAF tasked with taking on the large enemy fighter force relished the prospect of a good scrap. In the eyes of the RAF it was not so much a disadvantage of numbers, but a target-rich environment. The Spitfires attacked and soon the enemy fighters were seen spiralling towards a fiery death beneath the jungle canopy. One Spitfire pilot recalled:

The Zero had served the Japanese Air Force well over the years since Pearl Harbor, yet by 1943, the Zero was still the same aircraft it had been in 1941. The Zero had not been significantly upgraded to match the continually improved marks of British fighters, thus it was a relatively easy opponent for a pilot sitting in a decent fighter aircraft with some experience behind him, which we had. We had the Hawker Hurricane in action with us, but these aircraft were assigned to a reconnaissance role and were piloted by the men of the Indian Air Force. These men were exceptionally brave pilots, often overlooked in Second World War history. To do what they did in their outdated aircraft, outnumbered by their enemy which possessed the excellent Zero, was something quite exemplary.

Indeed, it was the brave pilots of the Indian Air Force in their Hurricanes who had the unenviable task of taking off time and time again in the face of quite overwhelming enemy opposition. In fact, when General Slim visited the squadron, the sombre announcement was made that the last patrol of Hurricanes on that particular occasion had been intercepted by Japanese Zeros which had resulted in the loss of all the Hurricanes. Yet the Sikh squadron leader, a personal friend of General Slim's, wasted no time in personally leading another patrol out to complete the mission. It was typical of the bravery of these fine men whose talents as airmen were no doubt down to their Sikh squadron leader's unorthodox methods. Slim recalled that the squadron leader was an absolute stickler for aerial discipline: if a pilot forgot to put his landing gear down on landing, it was said that he would take the unfortunate pilot behind a hut and give him a beating with a stick. However unorthodox this method was, it was noted that this squadron was efficient, happy and very gallant despite its technical disadvantages. The Hurricane pilots went through a torrid time against the Japanese – their worn-out, bullet-ridden aircraft flew out of theatre with bamboo skids in place of their tailwheels, with worn-out pilots at the controls. Many were of the opinion that little had been accomplished in the difficult aerial struggle with the Japanese, yet these frustrations and accompanying disappointments laid the foundations for the resurgence of Allied air domination in South-East Asia. Flying Officer Michael Read Wright recalls the arrival of the Supermarine Spitfire in the Asian theatre of operations:

> There was a sense of great relief and it was a huge morale-booster to hear the characteristic growl of Rolls-Royce Merlin engines in the distance, a sound that made the hairs on the back of one's neck stand on end. Then they came into view overheard: what a marvellous sight that was to behold. The Spitfire was a reassuring shape to see in the sky above; they circled for some minutes then one by one they came into land. We knew this meant the end for the Zero, as good an aircraft as it was – the Spitfire was exemplary; the Zero could not compete with a Spitfire. The aim then was to wipe the sky clear of the Japanese air force over Asia. In the first actual combats with the Japanese, it was like a game of cat and mouse. I wanted the Japanese pilot who

found himself in front of my guns to feel the fear that we had to contend with over the past months. He had no answer to my Spitfire; no matter how hard he turned he could not throw me off his tail – I had the better aeroplane and I could destroy him at my leisure. The second I lined him up in my sight I pressed the gun button; my 20mm cannon shells tore the Zero to shreds and it exploded into flames. I watched this cloud of debris fall into the jungle canopy below, followed by a plume of smoke. A Zero dived upon me, determined to get on my tail. I threw him off with ease and turned on him. I fired a two-second burst right into his port side as he was attempting to turn into me; he vanished in a sheet of flame and another enemy crashed to the jungle floor dead at his aircraft's controls. Now it was their turn to feel the frustration, humiliation and hopelessness of being thrown into combat against an opponent they would have no answer to.

Yes, it was a wonderful experience and the Spitfire adapted very well to the conditions overall. We all loved the Spitfire; she was a beautiful aeroplane, an absolute dream to fly and she possessed a vicious bite. The Hurricane wasn't a bad aeroplane; it was just not suited to combat in this particular environment and it lacked the cannon armament which our Spitfires had. The Zero was highly vulnerable to an eight-machine-gun burst from a Hurricane, but the problem was the Hurricane could not compete in terms of manoeuvrability with the Zero. In this battle speed and manoeuvrability were everything and the Spitfire gave us that edge tenfold. Later that evening, we all raised a glass to Reginald Mitchell the designer of that iconic fighter. I recall one of the boys remarking, 'Good old Mitch. Bless your soul, old boy!'

As the Arakan situation became clear to General Slim, who was recovering from his ninth daily dysentery injection of emetine, it was confirmed that the Japanese were attacking in considerable strength and had bypassed the 7th Division unobserved, something that angered Slim considerably, who had expected at least some prior warning of the enemy's movements. Not a man easily flustered, he quickly returned to headquarters where he telephoned General Christison. Christison knew little other than that Messervy's reserve brigade was engaged in heavy fighting with the enemy. The fighting was characteristically brutal, the Japanese attacking in force and pushing forward despite taking heavy casualties. The battle became known as the Battle of Admin Box. Brigadier Geoffrey Evans who had recently been appointed commander of the 9th Indian Infantry Brigade, 5th Indian Division, was ordered to make his way to Admin Box, assume command and hold the box against Japanese attack. Evans reinforced the defence of the box with the 2nd Battalion, West Yorkshire Regiment and 24th Mountain Artillery Regiment, Indian Army. A vital factor in the reinforcement operation was the two squadrons of M3 Lee tanks of the 25th Dragoons. The defenders were later joined by part of the 4th Battalion, 8th Gurkha Rifles, 89th Indian Infantry Brigade, 7th Indian Division, and also artillery of the 8th (Belfast) Heavy Anti-Aircraft Regiment, Royal Artillery, along with the 6th Medium Regiment Royal Artillery.

Evans organized the Admin Box into a defended position. The clearing area measured a bare 1,200 yards in diameter. Ammunition was piled at the foot of the western face of a central hillock, 150 feet high, which was named 'Ammunition Hill'. Major-General Mersservy reached the Admin Box, followed by several of his HQ personnel. They had made a precarious journey through the jungle in small groups through Japanese troop concentrations. Mersservy then left the defence of Admin Box to Evans while he concentrated on the re-establishment of controlling and directing the rest of the division.

Allied Douglas C-47 'Dakota' aircraft were then tasked with supplying the now cut-off troops. The Dakotas flew 714 sorties dropping some 2,300 tons of supplies. The first sorties met resistance from Japanese fighters, forcing some of the transport aircraft to turn back. However, the balance of power soon changed when three squadrons of Spitfires operating out of new airfields around Chittagong rapidly gained air superiority over the battlefield. Some sixty-five Japanese aircraft were quoted as being shot down or damaged for the loss of just three Spitfires. Several Hurricane fighter-bombers and some other Allied aircraft were lost, but whatever the true figures may have been, the Japanese were decisively routed from the area. The Japanese had failed to anticipate this logistical miracle, and while they would run short of supplies, the Indian formations could still fight on. The Japanese attempted to supply Sakurai Force with a mule train and Arakanese porters. They followed the same route of Sakurai's original infiltration but were ambushed in the jungle and all the supplies were captured as a result.

The fighting for the Admin Box witnessed some of the most determined Japanese aggression to date. Most of the fighting was of the kind the Japanese favoured most: close-in hand to hand. As a result, Japanese barbarism soon surfaced yet again when on the night of the 7 February, Japanese troops captured the main divisional dressing station. Thirty-five medical staff and patients were murdered in an orgy of sadism with bayonets and swords. Word of the incident reached the defenders and their resolve immediately hardened: they now understood quite clearly what would happen to them should they allow the position to fall to their enemy. The crowded nature of the defence meant casualties were high. Twice ammunition dumps were set ablaze and only the rapid reaction of the men nearby saved the post from disaster. The armour in the form of the M3 Lee tanks really came to the fore in the battle. The Japanese had no answer to the tanks especially once the ammunition for their few mountain artillery guns had run out.

On 14 February the Japanese carried forward an all-out do-or-die attack and succeeded in capturing one hill on the perimeter. It was a costly if short-lived victory as they were driven back off the hill the following day by the 2nd West Yorkshire Regiment with support from the M3 Lee tanks, the Yorkshires suffering heavy casualties in the process.

By 22 February starvation was setting in among the Japanese. Colonel Tanahashi, commanding officer of the Japanese 112th Infantry Regiment, responsible for providing the main body of the Sakurai Force, stated that his regiment had been reduced to 400 men out of an original strength of 2,150. Under these dire circumstances, Tanahashi refused to commit to further attacks. On 24 February – 19 February according to some sources – Tanahashi broke radio communication and withdrew without authorization. On 26 February, Major General Sakurai Tokutaró was left with no option but to abandon the operation.

Although total Allied casualties were significantly higher than the Japanese, the Japanese had abandoned many of their wounded troops, where they were left to die. Five thousand dead Japanese were counted on the battlefield that resembled a slaughterhouse. Flies and maggots fed on the corpses of the dead of both sides, yet for the first time in the Burma campaign, Japanese tactics, which in the past had served them so well, now counted for little: the tide was turning against the Japanese in Asia. More battles were to follow including Imphal and Kohima, but the fact that British and Indian troops had held and defeated a major Japanese attack for the first time proved invaluable for morale, and the news was widely broadcast around the world.

Private Robin Horsley, whom I had the pleasure of talking with in 1989, had fought with the West Yorkshire Regiment. He was a man who had talked very little of his war against the Japanese. His wife informed me prior to our meeting that Rob didn't talk easily about his experiences and to take it easy with him as he got upset easily. I understood the tact required when speaking to veterans, and understood perfectly his wife's concerns. I found Rob a typical old soldier; he was proud of his service and his part in the war and fetched his campaign medals to show me. He took a deep breath and recalled:

> That war against the savages, because that's what they all were in the Japanese army, was where I witnessed personally man's inhumanity to other men. I found their whole mentality difficult to understand; they killed unnecessarily on many occasions and killed without any remorse or mercy. In war and battle you expect to kill and to see other men being killed – that's all part of it, the fighting man knows that. The Japanese attacks against the place known as the Admin Box were very fierce. As many as we shot and killed more would come rushing at us. Some of them had swords raised above their heads, hacking and slashing anything in their way. It was madness. Even wounded Japs didn't just give up, and they would try and throw grenades at us. One chap I knew crawled across to a dying Jap and I remember thinking, 'What the hell are you doing?' He crawled over to the Jap, took out this knife and stabbed the Jap in the head with it, then he crawled calmly back across to us. He just said, 'You can't take any chances, even with a dead Jap.' And then he laughed. We had no feelings for them at all, even the wounded ones; we had learned from experience they were among the most devious and evil enemies you

could ever face. We didn't take any chances and if we were able, we killed any wounded Japs rather than waste any of our medical resources on them.

After the fighting had ended, we saw the state of the positions they had once occupied. The smell was atrocious, it was littered with rotten corpses of their dead, urine and faeces. What disturbed us most was that we found Japanese corpses that had flesh sliced off. It had been sliced off in a methodical manner, like how a butcher might carve a joint of meat. They had been eating their own dead as they were beginning to starve. This wasn't the first or last time I encountered these practices of cannibalism with Japanese soldiers; they did this frequently. Usually it was not permitted for a Jap to eat parts of another dead Jap, which was what one of the prisoners we captured told us. He said their commanding officer would turn a blind eye if they wanted to eat parts from dead Allied soldiers, but he would not tolerate them eating the flesh of their own dead. The whole thing disgusted me, it made me feel ill; they'd eat parts of corpses with rice. After the battle we walked around looking for anything we might take for a souvenir. Usually it was a flag or a bayonet or something. Sometimes we'd take a helmet or cut the insignia off their uniforms. We would search their pockets for anything of interest too. Often you would find a good luck charm, a photo of a woman or child, maybe even a letter. In that sense they were much like us, but in their instinct as soldiers they were ruthless and would murder medical staff and murder patients in their beds. Now it was their turn. That's how we looked at it; we had shown them they could be beaten, and we would beat them again and again until they were defeated.

After the incident at the medical aid post we were shocked, horrified and angry yet not surprised at their behaviour. For those who witnessed the scene in that aid post, me included, it made us angry, really angry. Some of the bodies had been decapitated with swords, or had their arms or legs chopped off. One of the medical examiners who saw the bodies of the murdered staff said that while they were being butchered they had most likely still been alive, the juxtaposition of the bodies and marks on their hands and arms had shown they had tried to fight off their attackers as they were being cleaved. One poor bloke turned to me and he said, 'Rob, in all my fucking years I've never seen anything like this. This is not the work of any human being, this is the work of evil, the devil.' Between us we had a code: if a Jap wanted to surrender, we would oblige him then we would quickly kill him if we could. It was the bloody officers that often got in the way of this. Them and their la-de-dah principles: 'Oh, no chaps we can't do things this way. It is awfully uncivilized, and I will court martial any chap caught killing Japanese prisoners.' That was the attitude with some of the officer class. Damn them. There were some that didn't care less what we did to the Japs; in fact one turned his back while I strangled one Japanese to death. I strangled him because when I looked through his pockets, I found a silver pocket watch which was inscribed with the words, 'To Alan, from your loving wife, Vera'. I thought, 'You bastard' and that was it. I knocked him down sat on his chest and I strangled the life from him. I took the pocket watch hoping to return it to whoever Alan was or his wife Vera back home. It took me a few years but eventually I was contacted by someone who knew who this chap was. He took it and returned it to his wife, Vera Higgins. Apparently, this Alan chap had been missing for some months; they never found his body. His wife Vera was a young woman, now a widow at just 23 years of age with no grave to visit. All she had was that watch which she gave to her husband before he had left for India a year or so before. It was just a token, something to remember her by. I know we did the same with their dead, we took things we wanted off them. I don't know, I guess that made me a hypocrite but that's war though for you.

I asked Rob if he had kept any of the souvenirs from the battles he had fought in, and he admitted that it was all gone now, most of it thrown out by his wife during house moves and clear-outs. He added,

'I don't think I would have wanted it now anyway. It would only have served as a reminder of times I would rather forget.' With the interview complete I shook Rob's hand and thanked him for taking the time to talk with me. As I left his wife said to me, 'Do you know, he's talked about things today that he has never talked about before, and we have been married now for over forty-five years. I hope it's got things off his mind as I think he needed it.' It just reaffirmed to me the importance of carrying out this kind of research, that someday I might be able to share with the world.

Chapter 11

Imphal

'When you go home, tell them of us and say,
For your tomorrow, we gave our today.'

The battles of Imphal and Kohima were two simultaneous actions which were to prove decisive in defeating the Japanese in the Far East while also curtailing any Japanese intentions of invading India. The Battle of Imphal takes its name from the city of Imphal, the capital of the state of Manipur in north-east India. The battle was fought from 8 March to 3 July 1944. Allied forces consisted of four infantry divisions, one armoured brigade and one parachute brigade. The Japanese had at their disposal three infantry divisions and one tank regiment. Commanding the British units were Field Marshal William Slim, General Sir Geoffrey Scoones and Air Marshal Sir John Baldwin, while the Japanese forces were under the command of Masakazu Kawabe and Mutaguchi Renya. Subhas Chandra Bose led the Indian National Army.

Bose, as discussed earlier in this book, is an interesting character, an Indian nationalist who became leader of the Indian National Army, an army of Indian soldiers sympathetic to the Japanese which then formed an allegiance with Imperial Japan and her Axis partner Nazi Germany. The INA – Azad Hind Fauj, or Indian Free Army – despised British colonial rule and fought against her colonial master. Bose made every effort to convince Indians to desert and join his INA force, yet many Indians disliked the man and treated him with contempt.

Japanese commander Mutaguchi was placed in command of his army in July 1943 and wasted no time in forcefully advocating an invasion of India. He felt that it was his personal destiny to win a decisive war for Japan, having been greatly goaded by the success of the Chindits in their attacks upon Japanese forces. He was keen to emulate the success of the Chindits, yet in the British propaganda there was never mention of the heavy losses that the Chindits suffered which may have misled Mutaguchi and his staff who would have been ignorant of the difficulties they would later face.

By the beginning of 1944 the tide was starting to turn against the Japanese on several fronts. They were losing ground in the campaigns of the Central and South-West Pacific; their merchant shipping was suffering under increasing attacks from Allied air and sea power. In South-East Asia the Japanese under difficult conditions had held their lines over the preceding year, yet the Allies were preparing several offensives from India and the Chinese province of Yunnan into Burma. The town of Imphal in Manipur, which lay on the frontier with Burma, grew into a significant Allied logistical hub, comprising airfields, encampments and supply storage areas. Imphal was also linked to an even larger base of even greater Allied logistical importance at Dimapur near the Brahmaputra River valley. A road ran for a hundred miles from this base through the steep and thickly forested Naga Hills.

The plan devised by Mutaguchi in his effort to capture Imphal would mean that his forces would sever all lines of Allied communications to the front in northern Burma, where the American-led Northern Combat Area Command was attempting to construct the Ledo Road to link India and China by land, and to the airfields supplying the Nationalist Chinese under Chiang Kai-shek via airlift over what was known as 'The Hump' – the Himalayas. Mutaguchi's plan was viewed with some concern by his superiors at Japanese Supreme Command South-East Asia and Southern Pacific, yet they were, after some aggressive and persistent persuasion from Mutaguchi, won over by his proposal. Finally, it was given approval by Japanese Prime Minister Hideki Tojo along with Imperial General Headquarters. The plan consisted of following objectives:

(a) The 33rd Infantry Division under the command of Lieutenant General Motoso Yanagida would surround and destroy the 17th Indian Division at Tiddim, then attack Imphal from the south.

(b) Yamamoto Force, formed from units detached from the Japanese 33rd and 15th Divisions, under Major General Tsunoru Yamamoto [commander of the 33rd Division Infantry Group] would destroy the 20th Indian Division at Tamu, then attack Imphal from the east. The force would be supported by the 14th Tank Regiment, equipped with 66 assorted tanks, under Lieutenant Colonel Nobuo Uedal, and the 3rd Heavy Artillery Regiment under Lieutenant Colonel Kazuo Mitsui.

(c) The 15th Infantry Division under Lieutenant General Masafumi Yamauchi would envelop Imphal from the north. (This division was still arriving from road-building duties in Thailand and was under strength at the start of the operation.)

(d) In a separate subsidiary operation, the 31st Infantry Division under Lieutenant General Kotoku Sato would isolate the Imphal–Dimapur road, and then advance to Dimapur.

Subhas Chandra Bose, leader of the Azad Hind/Indian National Army, was despondent at the lack of any meaningful role for his Indian Nationalist soldiers within Mutaguchi's plan and insisted that rather than his forces being used for reconnaissance and propaganda, they be allocated a substantial role in the coming operation. Considering Bose's protests, the Japanese agreed and subsequently the forces of the Azad Hind formed a substantial contribution to the Japanese commitment:

(e) The units of the 1st Division (initially the Subhas Brigade or 1st Guerrilla Regiment, less a battalion sent to the Arakan), would cover the left flank of 33rd Division's advance.

(f) The 2nd Guerrilla Regiment would later be attached to Yamamoto Force.

(g) The Special Services Group, redesignated the Dahadur Group, would act as scouts and pathfinders with the advanced Japanese units in the opening stages of the offensive, tasked with infiltrating British lines and encouraging units of the loyal British Indian Army to defect.

It appeared that Mutaguchi's divisional commanders had some reservations with the plan. Sato did not trust Mutaguchi's motives, and Yanagida was openly critical of his superior, even referring to him as 'a blockhead'. Their main arguments were based around the problems of supply. Mutaguchi had been slightly arrogant in the assumption that he could achieve success within a time scale of just three weeks, but adequate supplies after that period could only be obtained if the Japanese managed to capture Allied supply dumps, as the tropical rains that spring season would inevitably mean that supply routes from the Chindwin River would be impassable. Mutaguchi was taking a huge gamble: the Japanese had made many such gambles in the past, yet now they could not be relied upon owing to near-total Allied air superiority combined with the greatly improved morale and training of the British and Indian troops.

Mutaguchi had the wildly ambitious idea of utilizing 'Genghis Khan' rations, which involved driving herds of buffalo and cattle rounded up throughout northern Burma across the Chindwin as readily available rations on the hoof. The shortcomings of such an ambitious endeavour were that many of the animals died from a lack of forage, and what meat was taken from them rotted miles from the troops they were intended to supply.

As the campaign advanced, other weaknesses became glaringly apparent. The Japanese were of the view that the British would be unable to use their armour in the form of tanks on the steep jungle terrain around Imphal. They left behind much of their field artillery as it was felt these guns might impinge on any rapid tactical manoeuvres which may be necessary at a moment's notice. This was truly foolhardy as these weapons formed the greater part of their anti-tank capability. As a result, Japanese troops would have little protection against the Allied armour pitched against them.

Arrogance again would be one of Mutaguchi's greatest failings. He had based much of his planning on his experiences in the campaigns in Malaya and Singapore and the Japanese conquest of Burma. He made the error of underestimating his British and Indian foes as inferior. Those Allied forces he would now be facing were nothing like those he had faced in early 1942, with troops inadequately trained, equipped and led. The Allies by now had largely overcome, through hard experience, the administrative and organizational issues which had plagued them during their early efforts in Burma, and Allied troops in theatre now were far better trained and motivated than their Japanese enemy.

Imphal itself was held by IV Corps, under the command of Lieutenant-General Geoffrey Scoones, and part of the Fourteenth Army under Lieutenant-General William Slim. Due to the fact that the Allies were planning to go over to the offensive on their own initiative, corps units were thrown forward almost to the Chindwin River. There were concerns that they were too widely separated and could become isolated and surrounded. The Allied order of battle consisted of the following:

(a) 20th Indian Infantry Division under Major-General Douglas Gracey occupied Tamu, 110 kilometres (68 miles) south-east of Imphal. This division was untested in battle but was well prepared.

(b) 17th Indian Infantry Division under Major-General 'Punch' Cowan occupied Tiddim, 243 kilometres (151 miles) south of Imphal, at the end of a long and precarious line of communication. The division, which comprised two brigades only, had seen intermittent combat since December 1941.

(c) 23rd Indian Infantry Division under Major-General Ouvry Roberts was acting as a reserve force in and around Imphal. The division had served on the Imphal front for two years, and was severely under strength as a result of endemic diseases such as malaria and typhus.

(d) 50th Indian Parachute Brigade under Brigadier Maxwell Hope-Thompson was positioned north of Imphal, conducting advanced jungle training.

(e) 254th Indian Tank Brigade under Brigadier Reginald Scoones was stationed in and around Imphal.

Through the Allied intelligence network, it was soon revealed that the Japanese planned to imminently launch a major offensive. General Slim and Brigadier Scoones planned to withdraw their forward divisions to bring them onto the Imphal plain to force the Japanese to fight at the end of an overstretched and difficult line of communication. In the fog of war that often transpires, the two Allied commanders misjudged the date on which the Japanese intended to launch their attack, and the strength they would allocate towards their objectives. The Japanese troops began crossing the Chindwin River on 8 March. Scoones gave his forward divisions the order to withdraw to Imphal only on 13 March.

The 20th Indian Division held Tamu near the Chindwin, as well as Moreh a short distance to the north, where a large supply dump had been established. On 20 March, there was an engagement between six Allied Lee tanks of the 3rd Carabiniers and six Japanese Type 95 Ha-Go tanks leading Yamamoto's advance from the south. The lightweight

Japanese tanks proved no match for their Allied counterparts and were soon destroyed. Major-General Douglas Gracey was reluctant to retreat, but on 25 March he was ordered to detach a portion of his division to provide a reserve for IV Corps. This move left the division in too weak a position to hold Tamu and Moreh, and they withdrew to the Shenam Saddle, a complex of hills through which the Imphal–Tamu road ran. The supply dump at Moreh was set ablaze, and 200 cattle there were slaughtered. The division fell back without difficulty, mainly due to two of Yamamoto's battalions from the Japanese 15th Division – 11/51 Regiment and III/60 Regiment – being delayed at Indaw in the north of Burma by the Chindits, an action which meant this Japanese force was unable to intervene.

Farther south, the 17th Indian Division was cut off by the Japanese 33rd Division. Patrols from the division and from V Force – an irregular force of locally raised levies and guerrillas – warned Cowan of a Japanese force advancing against the rear of the division as early as 8 March, allowing Cowan to regroup the division to defend its rear. On 13 March the Japanese 215th Regiment attacked a supply dump at Milestone 109, some twenty miles behind Cowan's leading outposts, while the Japanese 214th Regiment seized Tongzang and a ridge named Tuitum Saddle across the road a few miles behind the 17th Indian Division's main position.

The Indian division began withdrawing on 14 March. At Tuitum Saddle, on 15 March, the Japanese 214th Regiment was unable to dig in sufficiently before coming under attack from the 48th Indian Infantry Brigade. Subsequently, during the fierce fighting that ensued the Japanese suffered heavy casualties and were forced from the road. Gahor Padur, one of the Indian troops of the 48th Indian Infantry Brigade, recalled:

> Our fire was most effective; we had learned to fire heavily into the Japanese who attempted suicidal charges into rifle-, light mortar and machine-gun fire. All around they fell in masses and we then drove them away at bayonet point. As I went forward, I stabbed at any Japanese with my bayonet to finish them off, I didn't wish to be shot in the back having got this far against what was a truly godless, ruthless enemy. One Japanese tried to surrender to me – they sometimes

did this but had grenades with their pins pulled out which they released as soon you got near them. I shot him without hesitation, and I moved onward.

Farther north, on 18 March, the Japanese captured the depot at Milestone 109, which was a short-lived success as Indian troops recaptured the depot on 25 March. Cowan had taken steps to secure the most vulnerable point in the rear of his division, the bridge which spanned the Manipur River. The division's rearguard crossed the river safely on 26 March, then blew the bridge to deny the enemy access across the river. The division was able to remove most of the vehicles, food and ammunition from the depot at Milestone 109 before continuing their retreat. Both the Indian division and the Japanese suffered heavy casualties. Commander of the Japanese 33rd Division, General Yanagida, was now very concerned, apparently unnerved by a garbled radio message that implied one of his regiments had been wiped out at Tongzang. He was therefore reluctant to press any pursuit of the 17th Division, and advanced overcautiously in spite of reprimands from Mutaguchi.

Scoones on the other hand, had nevertheless been forced into sending the bulk of his only reserve, the 23rd Indian Infantry Division, to the aid of the 17th Division. The two divisions, assisted by supply drops from Allied aircraft, made their way back to the Imphal Plain, which they reached by 4 April.

Meanwhile, Imphal had been left vulnerable to the Japanese 15th Division. The only force left covering the northern approaches to the base, the Indian 50th Parachute Brigade, had experienced a rough time at the Battle of Sangshak at the hands of a regiment from the Japanese 31st Division which had been on its way to Kohima. The Japanese 60th Regiment cut the main road a few miles north of Imphal on 28 March, while the 51st Regiment advanced on Imphal from the north-east, through the valley of the Iril River and a track from Litan, twenty-three miles north-east of Imphal.

The earlier diversionary attack launched by the Japanese 55th Division in Arakan had already failed. Admiral Louis Mountbatten, Commander-in-Chief Allied South East Asia Command, had taken steps to secure aircraft normally assigned to the 'Hump'. Field Marshal Slim was able to use these to move the battle-hardened 5th Indian Infantry Division, including all of its artillery and first-line transport (Jeeps and mules), by air from Arakan to the Central Front. This move was made in just eleven days, a remarkable feat of logistics. One brigade and a mountain artillery regiment deployed to Dimapur in the Brahmaputra valley, but the other two brigades, the field artillery and the divisional Headquarters went to Imphal. The leading troops of the division were in action north and east of Imphal on 3 April.

On the Japanese left flank, the Indian National Army's Subhas Brigade, led by Shah Nawaz Khan, reached the edge of the Chin Hills below Tiddim and Fort White at the end of March. From this position the 2nd Battalion sent companies to relieve Japanese forces at Falam and to Hakha, from where in turn Khan sent out patrols and laid ambushes for the Chin guerrillas under the command of a British officer, Lieutenant-Colonel Oates, taking a number of prisoners. In mid-May, a force under Khan's adjutant, Mahboob 'Boobie' Ahmed, attacked and captured the hilltop fortress of Klang Klang. The 3rd Battalion meanwhile moved to Fort White-Tongzang area in premature anticipation of the destruction of Major-General Frank Messervy's 7th Indian Infantry Division in the Arakan, which would allow it to receive volunteers.

During the early phases of the offensive, the Bahadur Group of the Indian National Army apparently achieved some success in inducing British Indian soldiers to desert, though, to their credit, most the British Indian soldiers refused, still preferring death to betrayal.

From the beginning of April, the Japanese attacked the Imphal Plain from several directions: the 33rd Division attacked from the south at Bishenpur, where they cut a secondary track from Silchar into the plain. An Allied commando raid had earlier destroyed a suspension bridge, thus making the Silchar track unpassable. The 17th and 23rd Indian Divisions were regrouping after their retreat, while Bishenpur was held only by the 32nd Indian Infantry Brigade (detached from the 20th Division). The Japanese advanced through the hills to the west of Bishenpur, almost isolating the British in the village, but suffered heavily from British artillery fire. Their leading troops were halted by lack of supplies some ten miles from Imphal. Other Japanese forces advancing directly up to the Tiddim–Imphal road were halted at Potsangbam two miles south of Bishenpur as troops of 17th Indian Division rejoined the battle.

Yanagida, the Japanese divisional commander, had already reduced Mutaguchi to a man raging with frustration over his overt caution.

As tensions between the two reached breaking point, he was finally relieved of his command at the end of the month.

Yamamoto Force attacked the Shenam Saddle, defended by the main body of the Indian 20th Division, on the main road from Tamu into Imphal. This was the only metalled road the Japanese could use, and it was vital for them to break through to allow Yamamoto's tanks and heavy artillery to attack the main defences around Imphal itself. Only a few miles north of the saddle was Palel airfield, one of only two all-weather airfields on the plain, and vital to the defenders.

A Japanese attack up the road on 4 April was disjointed; the infantry was not ready to take part and twelve Japanese tanks were caught exposed on the road by British anti-tank guns which took a heavy toll on the Japanese armour. Gerald Sturness one of the anti-tank gunners in action that day, recalled:

> It was great getting to grips with their tanks. The Jap tanks were very poorly armoured, and they were still using the same outdated armour that they began the war with. It was a turkey shoot in every way. It was 'bang' and you would put a round into one tank, then go to the next 'bang' and the things just burst into flames; they were death traps. Sometimes you would see their crews scrambling out through the crew hatches on the tops and they would be machine-gunned before they'd even dropped down off the tanks.

From 8 to 22 April, there was heavy fighting for the five peaks which commanded the road east of the saddle. The Japanese were successful in capturing a number of them, but Indian and British counterattacks regained possession of those initially lost. As one would expect, casualties were high on both sides.

Having failed to break through using the road, Yamamoto sent some of his troops through the rough terrain to the north of the saddle to raid Palel airfield. The Indian National Army's Gandhi Brigade or 2nd Guerrilla Regiment, of two battalions led by Inayat Kiyani, took part in this attack. On 28 April, they attacked Palel. They made an attempt to persuade some of the Indian defenders to surrender, but the defenders rallied together after some initial hesitation. Another Indian National Army detachment carried out demolitions around Palel but withdrew after failing to rendezvous with Japanese units in the area. The Gandhi Brigade was critically short of rations, having brought forward only one day's supplies; it also lost 250 of its number to artillery fire after they pulled back from Palel.

The Japanese 15th Division encircled Imphal from the north. Its 60th Regiment captured a British supply dump at Kanglatongbi on the main Imphal–Dimapur road a few miles north of Imphal, but the depot had been emptied of food and ammunition.

A battalion of the Japanese 51st Regiment, under the command of Colonel Kimio Omoto, seized the vital Nungshigum Ridge, a feature which overlooked the main airstrip at Imphal. This proved a major threat to IV Corps and on the 13 April, the 5th Indian Division counterattacked with the support of air strikes, massed artillery and the M3 Lee tanks of B Squadron, 3rd Carabiniers. The Japanese had theorized that the slopes would be too difficult for armour to negotiate. The M3 Lee tanks had never previously attempted to climb such steep a gradient in combat but they performed admirably to the horror of the Japanese, who possessed few effective anti-tank weapons. Subsequently, the Japanese were driven from the ridge suffering heavy casualties in the process. The Allied force had also suffered heavily during the fighting: every officer of the Carabiniers and the attacking infantry, the 1st Battalion, 17th Dogra Regiment, was killed. Sunil Johur, a soldier of the 17th Dogra Regiment, recalled in vivid detail some of the action:

> The Japanese had no answer to the tanks. The tanks pushed forward clumsily at first up what was a very steep slope, yet they overcame this obstacle. Any Japanese that lay in the path of those tanks were driven over and crushed to death; I saw it with my own eyes. One of the things I recall most of all is how Japanese soldiers would spring up from nowhere; they would surprise us like corpses jumping out from the ground. You would be looking around everywhere and there would be nothing, then you would look again and there would be a Japanese in full charge running at you with his bayonet. You would shoot him dead, watch him fall, but I always shot him again in the head if I could to make sure he wasn't playing dead. I learned this lesson from the Japanese. A friend was killed while investigating the body

of a Japanese he had thought he had killed. The Japanese lay quite still with a grenade in his hands. As soon as my friend went to him and turned him over the Japanese detonated his grenade, killing my friend. That was a very sad time as we had been friends for a very long time, since childhood. How these Japanese managed to get so close I don't know. They often crawled through perimeters unseen and would sneak up with grenades or stab a man with his sword or bayonet. Another man I knew was stabbed in the neck as he was walking. They warned us to be aware in heavy jungle terrain, of solitary enemy waiting for a chance to kill or wound us. This one Japanese, we did not see him, and he was very well camouflaged. As we walked by, he thrust out his rifle stabbing my friend through the neck. It was a fatal wound and my friend died there on the spot. The Japanese was dragged away and beaten to death with rifle butts and we left him there for the ants to feed on. This may sound barbaric to people today, but it was war at its worst.

By 1 May, all Japanese attacks had ground to a halt. General Slim and Brigadier Scoones began a counteroffensive against the Japanese 15th Division. This was the weakest of the enemy formations and, if defeated, the siege would be broken, once Kohima was retaken. The Allied counterattack was somewhat sluggish due to a few factors. The monsoon rains had arrived which severely hampered logistics operations which were tough enough under normal conditions. Also, IV Corps was suffering from some shortages. Although food rations and reinforcements were supplied to Imphal by air, artillery ammunition was in short supply and had to be conserved.

The 5th Indian Division, joined by the 89th Indian Infantry Brigade which was flown in to replace the brigade sent to Kohima, and the 23rd Indian Division (later replaced by the 20th Division) attempted to wrench the steep ridges such as the Mapao Spur held by the Japanese, which were found to be characteristically impregnable. One of the problems faced by the Allies was the ineffectiveness of their artillery due to the geography of the target areas. It was unable to place high explosive onto Japanese positions dug in on the reverse slopes. The only way the Japanese could be eliminated from these positions was by troops storming them. Troops often succeeded in taking the summits of the ridges, only to be beaten back by heavy Japanese fire from the reverse slope positions. IV Corps regrouped. The 23rd Indian Division took over the defence of the Shenam Saddle, while, from the end of the May, the 5th Division concentrated on pushing north from Sengmai up the main road through Kanglatongi. The 20th Indian Division advanced along tracks following the Iril River toward Litan and Ukhrul, threatening to sever the Japanese 15th Division's lines of communication.

At this time the Japanese found themselves at the pinnacle of their endurance. Neither the 31st Division which was fighting at Kohima nor the 15th had received adequate supplies since the offensive began: the Japanese troops were now starving. Lieutenant General Sato, commander of the 31st Division, had no other option other than to allow his troops to retreat so as they could find some food. This move then allowed the Indian XXXIII Corps to drive the Japanese from Kohima and advance south.

The troops of the Japanese 15th Division, scavenging in local villages and not content with stealing the locals' meagre food supplies, often ended their jungle forays with their popular sport of rape, sadism and murder. As they ransacked villages for food, young women and children were raped and tortured prior to being shot or bayoneted. Usually the men were rounded up, tied to trees and used for live bayonet practice. It was a wholly unnecessary course of action as most of the inhabitants of these villages offered no resistance to the heavily armed Japanese soldiers. The conduct of the Japanese was born purely out of some malicious pleasure. Sunil Johur believes the reason behind their barbarity was their anger and frustration at being defeated. He told me that sometimes Japanese prisoners were handed over to the villagers themselves where retribution was swift:

> This was not meant to be the course of action we should have taken. All Japanese prisoners it was stated should be taken away where they could then be questioned for any intelligence. The jungle war quickly evolved into one of savagery and I blame the Japanese for this happening. Yes, we did hand one Japanese over to some villagers, and he was sadistically killed by them. But we felt in some small way the villagers had received some justice for the rape and

murder of their womenfolk by venting their rage upon this prisoner. The Japanese had no notion of hearts and minds and were soon despised by all; that I would say was one of their many failings in the conduct of their war in Asia.

Mutaguchi dismissed the mortally ill Yamauchi, yet this did nothing to resolve the military situation for the Japanese. After driving rearguards from the Miyazaki Group (an independent detachment from the 31st Division) and the 60th Regiment from their delaying positions on the Dimapur–Imphal road, the leading troops of IV Corps and XXXIII Corps met at Milestone 109, ten miles north of Imphal, and on the 22 June the siege of Imphal was lifted.

To the south of Imphal, the 17th Indian Division had moved back into the line, facing the Japanese 33rd Division. During the first half of May, there were several Japanese air attacks on Bishenpur, and heavy fighting for the village of Potsangbam two miles to the south, where the Allies lost twelve of their tanks. The surviving crews of the 3rd Carabiniers were later flown out of Imphal to be reconstituted in India.

Major-General Cowan planned to break the deadlock on this front by sending the 48th Indian Infantry Brigade on a wide left-hook manoeuvre into the Japanese division's rear while the 63rd Indian Infantry Brigade attacked them from the front. The Japanese temporary commander was its chief of staff, Major-General Tetsujiro Tanaka. Tanaka planned at the same time to infiltrate through the 17th Indian Division's front to seize vital objectives in the middle of the Indian positions. Both moves were to be launched almost simultaneously.

The Gurkhas of the 48th Indian Brigade cut the road behind the Japanese on 18 May, but the 63rd Indian Brigade was unable to break through to them, thus the 48th Brigade had no option other than to fight their way through the Japanese positions to rejoin the division, suffering heavy casualties as a result. Gurkha Hidip Saakar recalled that particular action:

It was what the English called 'crazy stuff' yet it was a nightmare. The Japanese were everywhere and we went right through them, shooting with our rifles and hacking with our kukris. Most of the way we fought was hand to hand.

A Japanese was screaming at me with a grenade in his hand. I cut his hand off and the hand dropped to the ground still clutching the grenade. It was a case of fire some shots, move forward, check how clear the way ahead is, then move forward again. The Japanese would run out at us with their bayonets and we would shoot them dead or kill them with our kukris. Any Japanese in holes in the ground were easily dispatched with a kukri, grenade or shot from a rifle. The Japanese feared the kukri. People ask me did I collect any ears [he laughs]; I say to them no, I had no time to collect ears – there was far too much danger of being killed. We lost a lot of men; from the corners of my eyes I saw men dropping down dead to the ground.

Meanwhile some of Tanaka's troops – the 214th Regiment – were able to capture hills close to 17th Division's HQ on 20 May. Due to the incursion into their own rear, the Japanese were unable to reinforce their forward troops, and over the week that followed the isolated Japanese troops were driven from their positions in the centre of the Indian division. Many were annihilated as they withdrew.

Lieutenant General Nobuo Tanaka took over command of the 33rd Division on 22 May. Tanaka was an aggressive, forceful individual and immediately ordered repeated attacks which effectively reduced much of his strength to mere handfuls of men. In June Tanaka received reinforcements in the form of a regiment from the 53rd Division, and a detachment from the 14th Tank Regiment. Tanaka utilized these in yet another attack which, although initially successful, took heavy casualties from Allied artillery fire.

By the end of June, the Japanese 33rd Division had suffered such a high rate of casualties that it could no longer contribute further to the campaign. Yamamoto Force had also taken a beating, yet prior to withdrawing, they launched two modest raids on Palel Airfield in the first week of July. Allied casualties were light, with several parked aircraft destroyed.

The INA contribution proved largely inconclusive. Towards the end of May, the INA's 1st and 2nd Guerrilla Regiments – the latter under the command of Malik Munawar Khan Awan – were redirected to Kohima. The INA moved north across the Japanese rear but by the time they reached Ukhrul, the Japanese had already begun to withdraw. The INA decided to attack Imphal instead and in doing so suffered heavy losses along with some desertions. Most INA deserters were held in utter contempt by the Indian soldiers of the Allied forces. Few wanted anything to do with them as they were regarded as traitors and partly to blame for the Japanese atrocities. Sunil Johur recalls of these men:

> To us these men were nothing other than rats who had abandoned their yellow masters. These traitors had sided with the Japanese and were in my opinion guilty of the war crimes committed in Asia. They had served the Japanese and many of us felt they were as responsible for the terrible things the Japanese had done. These men were guilty by association and should have been executed, but no, they were not. We didn't trust any of them and we didn't speak to any of them; we eyed them with contempt. In our eyes they were no longer Indian, and they belonged to the yellow enemy.

The Japanese had realized that the operation would have to be broken off as early as May. Lieutenant General Hikosaburo Hata, Vice-Chief of the General Staff, had made a tour of inspection of Southern Army's headquarters in late April. Upon his return to Tokyo, he reported pessimistically on the outcome of the operation at a large staff meeting to Japanese Prime Minister Hideki Tojo, but Tojo dismissed his concerns. Messages were sent from Imperial Headquarters, urging that the operation was to continue to the end.

Lieutenant General Kawabe travelled north from Rangoon to ascertain the situation for himself. On 23 May several officers whom he interviewed expressed confidence in success providing adequate reinforcements could be supplied. Yet, they made no mention of the heavy losses in manpower nor the seriousness of the situation overall. At a meeting between Mutaguchi and Kawabe on 6 June both used *haragei*, an unspoken form of communication using gesture, expression and tone of voice, to convey their concerns that success was impossible: neither wished to bear the responsibility of ordering a retreat.

Mutaguchi ordered the Japanese 31st Division, which had retreated from Kohima when threatened with starvation, to join the 15th Division in a renewed attack on Imphal from the north. Neither division obeyed its orders, being in no condition to comply. When he realized this, Mutaguchi finally ordered the offensive to be broken off on 3 July. The Japanese, virtually reduced to a rabble, fell back to the Chindwin. They abandoned their artillery, transport and many of their own soldiers who were too badly wounded or sick to walk. The Allies recovered Tamu at the end of July where, to their horror, it was found to contain 550 unburied rotting Japanese corpses. A hundred dying Japanese soldiers were found among this mountain of bodies. It was described as 'an unholy spectacle' by one witness.

Chapter 12

Kohima

Kohima is a place unfamiliar to many, especially those unacquainted with the battles fought against the Japanese in the Far East during the Second World War. However, its importance in the defeat of the Japanese in the Asian theatre of war cannot be emphasized enough. To the Japanese Kohima possessed great strategic importance within the wider context of the 1944 Chindwin offensive. At Kohima Ridge lay the pass that offered the Japanese the best route from Burma into India. Through it ran the road that was the main supply route between the base at Dimapur in the Brahmaputra valley and Imphal, where the British and Indian troops of IV Corps – consisting of the 17th, 20th and 23rd Indian Infantry Divisions – faced the main Japanese offensive.

Kohima Ridge itself runs roughly north–south. The road from Dimapur to Imphal climbs to its northern end and runs along its eastern face. In 1944, Kohima was the administrative centre of Nagaland. The Deputy Commissioner was Charles Pawsey whose bungalow stood on the hillside at a bend in the road, with its well-manicured gardens, tennis court and clubhouse situated on terraces above. Although some terraces around the village were cleared for cultivation, the steep slopes of the ridge consisted of dense jungle. North of the ridge lay the heavily populated area known as the Naga Village, crowned by Treasury Hill and Church Knoll, the latter taking its name from the Baptist missionaries who had been active in Nagaland over the preceding half-century.

South and west of Kohima Ridge were GPT Ridge and the jungle-covered Aradura Spur. The various British and Indian service troop encampments in the area gave their names to the features which were to prove important in the Kohima battle, for example, Field Supply Depot became FSD Hill or merely FSD. The Japanese would later assign their own code-names to the features; for example, Garrison Hill to the Japanese became known as Inu (dog) and Kuki Piquet as Saru (monkey).

Prior to the arrival of the 161st Indian Brigade, the only combat troops in the Kohima region were the newly formed 1st Battalion, the Assam Regiment plus a few platoons from 3rd (Naga Hills) Battalion of the paramilitary Assam Rifles. In late March the 161st Brigade deployed to Kohima, but Major-General Ranking ordered them back to Dimapur, as it was initially believed that Dimapur had more strategic significance. Kohima was regarded as little more than a roadblock, while Dimapur was the railhead where the bulk of Allied war material were stored. Field Marshal Slim feared that the Japanese might leave only a detachment to contain the garrison of Kohima while the main body of the 31st Division moved by tracks to the east to attack Dimapur.

To Slim's relief, Japanese Lieutenant General Kotoku Sato concentrated on capturing Kohima. Earlier in the siege, on 8 April, Mutaguchi ordered Sato to send a detachment to advance on Dimapur. Sato unwillingly dispatched a battalion of the 138th Regiment but a few hours later Mutaguchi's superior, Lieutenant General Masakasu Kawabe, commander of Burmese Area Army, vetoed the move. In order to concentrate on the relief of Imphal, Slim chose to gamble that the Indian 5th Division could hold Kohima by themselves, though he knew that if the Japanese took Kohima, they would be able to sever the strategically vital Assam railroad at Dimapur, which would cut off the Fourteenth Army from its main source of supplies.

As the right wing and centre formations of the Japanese 31st Division approached Jessami, thirty miles to the east of Kohima, elements of the Assam Regiment fought delaying actions against them commencing 1 April. Nevertheless, the men in the forward positions were soon overrun, forcing the Assam Regiment to withdraw. By the night of 3 April, Miyazaki's troops reached the outskirts of the Naga Village and began probing Kohima from the south.

Stopford's Corps Headquarters took over responsibility for the front from Ranking on 3 April. The next day, he ordered the 161st Indian Brigade to advance to Kohima again, but only one battalion, the 4th Battalion, Queen's Own Royal West Kent Regiment under the command of Lieutenant-Colonel John Laverty, and a company of the 4th Battalion, 7th Rajput Regiment that arrived in Kohima before the Japanese cut the road west of Kohima Ridge. Besides these troops from the 161st Brigade, the garrison consisted of a raw battalion – the Shere Regiment – from the Royal Nepalese Army, some companies from the Burma Regiment, some of the Assam Regiment which had retired to Kohima Ridge plus various detachments of convalescent and line-of-communication troops. The garrison had at its disposal around 2,500 troops, of which around 1,000 were non-combatants and were commanded by Colonel Hugh Richards, who had formerly served with the Chindits.

The siege began on 6 April. The garrison on Kohima Ridge was subjected to a horrifying and persistent barrage of Japanese artillery and mortar fire. Much of the fire coming down on the garrison was from their own weapons which the Japanese forces had captured at Sangshak and numerous other Allied depots. Under the intensity of the Japanese onslaught, the garrison was steadily driven into a small perimeter on Garrison Hill. They had artillery support from the main body of the 161st Brigade, who were themselves cut off some two miles away at Jotsoma. At Sangshak the troops were very short of drinking water. The water supply point was on GPT Ridge, which had been captured by the Japanese on the first day of the siege. Some defenders were unable to retreat to other positions on the ridge and instead withdrew to Dimapur. Canvas water tanks on FSD and at the Indian General Hospital had neither been filled nor dug in to protect them from fire. While a small spring was discovered on the north side of Garrison Hill, it could be reached only at night. Medical dressing stations were exposed to Japanese fire, and wounded troops were often hit again by shrapnel while awaiting treatment.

Some of the heaviest fighting took place at the northern end of Kohima Ridge, around the Deputy Commissioner's bungalow and tennis court, in what became known as the Battle of the Tennis Court. The tennis court became a no-man's land, with the Japanese and the defenders of Kohima on opposite sides, yet so close to each other that grenades could easily be thrown between the trenches. American historians Allan Millet and Williamson Murray said that 'nowhere in World War Two – even on the Eastern Front in Russia – did the combatants fight with more mindless savagery than those at Kohima Ridge'.

In 2015, Kohima Ridge veteran, 94-year-old Roy Welland, spoke of the hell of the Kohima battle. Although fought seventy years before, he admitted that every time he thought about it, he would break out in a cold sweat. Roy had lost around seventy of his comrades during the battle and suffered nightmares ever since. He recalled in a press interview that year:

I can bring it forward and I can push it to the back of my mind, but I can never forget it. I can't explain why but it was pretty rough, and there was a lot of hand-to-hand fighting. Kohima was the worst. I had nightmares about it long after the battle and long after I had come out of the army. I used to sweat like a pig just talking about it. You were stepping over bodies all over the place, just lying around, and the smell alone made you feel sick. You did everything in your trousers that you could think of – that's crude but it's true. I don't care what anybody says, you did. But you did think to yourself, 'I don't want to die yet.' We were told to hang on and let them [the Japs] charge at us, with these Japanese officers screaming their heads off like maniacs. Yes, we hated them, of course we did, but you've got to hate because how could you stick a bayonet in a man if you didn't hate him? One Japanese soldier rushed at me. I was able to take him. I was not happy about it as it was the first time I had ever killed a man with my bayonet. After that first time it was not a problem and I killed two or three more after that with my bayonet. But seeing a man down on the ground, lying there screaming his head off because you are bayoneting him in the guts – that's the worst place you can ever stab a man with a bayonet. But then again, it's the best place because it stops him altogether. It's either you or him. Today I shed a tear about it when I think of it, but that's because I didn't want to have to do it, yet I had to do it. Once you had done it, you could go on and do it again and again, and it was just like everything else. That is how I looked at it. Do I feel any sense of guilt today? No, there is no guilt. I did what I had to do, and I have no regrets for having done it. It is not human to kill each other if you have been brought up right. You are brought up to respect people and help each other, not go around killing each other. I am not proud of it; far from it. But it had to be done otherwise I would not be here, now would I?

Roy Welland's experiences are typical of many veterans of Kohima, an experience many refer to as 'hell'.

On the night of 17/18 April, the Japanese finally captured the Deputy Commissioner's bungalow area. Other Japanese forces took Kuki Picquet, effectively cutting the garrison in half. The defenders' situation was desperate, but the Japanese did not follow up by attacking Garrison Hill as by now they were exhausted by hunger and the intensity of the fighting. When dawn broke, troops of the 161st Indian Brigade arrived to relieve the garrison. The 161st Indian Brigade arrived to witness scenes from hell itself. Kohima Ridge resembled a slaughterhouse. All around lay body parts and blood-soaked corpses of both Japanese and Allied soldiers. Trees had been torn apart by mortar and artillery fire, the buildings ruined and the ground a moonscape of shell craters. For those who survived the battle, Kohima would be an event that would haunt their memories for the rest of their lives, yet the nightmare was not over.

Under the cover of darkness, the wounded who numbered some 300, were brought out under fire. Although contact had been established, it took a further twenty-four hours to fully secure the road between Jotsoma and Kohima. During 19 April and into the early hours of 20 April the British 6th Brigade replaced the original garrison and at 0600 hours, the garrison commander, Colonel Richards, handed over command of the area. 6th Brigade's observers were taken aback by the condition of the garrison; one battle hardened officer remarked: 'They looked like aged bloodstained scarecrows, dropping with fatigue; the only clean thing about them was their weapons, and they smelt of blood, sweat and death.'

Miyazaki continued to try and capture Garrison Hill, with heavy fighting for this feature for several more nights, with heavy casualties on both sides. The Japanese positions on Kuki Picquet were only fifty yards from Garrison Hill, and fighting was subsequently hand to hand. On the other flank of Garrison Hill, on the night of 26/27 April, a British attack recaptured the clubhouse above the Deputy Commissioner's bungalow, which overlooked most of the Japanese centre. The Japanese reorganized for defence: their left-hand force under Miyazaki held Kohima Ridge with four battalions; divisional headquarters under Sato himself and the Centre Force under Colonel Shiraishi held Naga Village with another four battalions. The much smaller Right Force held villages to the north and east.

To support their attack against the Japanese position, the British had amassed thirty-eight 3.7-inch mountain howitzers, forty-eight

25-pounder field guns and two 5.5-inch medium guns. The RAF provided Hawker Hurricane fighter-bombers of 34 Squadron along with a number of Vultee Vengeance dive-bombers of 84 Squadron. These aircraft were tasked with bombing and strafing of the Japanese positions. The Japanese could only oppose the Allied force with seventeen light mountain artillery guns, with woefully inadequate supplies of ammunition. Nevertheless, progress on part of the British was slow. Tanks could not easily be used, and the Japanese occupied bunkers which were very deeply dug in, well concealed and mutually supporting.

While the British 6th Brigade defended Garrison Hill, the other two brigades of 2nd Division attempted to outflank both ends of the Japanese position, in Naga Village to the north and on GPT Ridge to the south. The monsoon having broken meant that the steep slopes became strength-sapping mud that bogged down any attempted movement and weather conditions made general supply extremely difficult in places. The British 4th Brigade had to physically cut steps out of hillsides and fabricate handrails in order to make any progress. On 4 May, the British 5th Brigade secured a foothold in the outskirts of Naga Village but was counterattacked and driven back. On the same day the British 4th Brigade, having made a long flanking march around Mount Pulebadze to approach Kohima Ridge from the south-west, attacked GPT Ridge in driving rain and managed to capture part of the ridge by surprise, yet was unable to secure the entire ridge. Two successive commanders of the British 4th Brigade were killed in the close-range fighting on the ridge.

Both outflanking moves having failed because of the terrain and the weather, the British 2nd Division concentrated on attacking Japanese positions along Kohima Ridge from 4 May onwards. Fire from Japanese posts on the reverse slope of GPT Ridge repeatedly caught British troops attacking Jail Hill in the flank, inflicting heavy casualties and preventing them from taking the hill for a week. However, the various positions were slowly taken. Jail Hill, together with Kuki Picquet, FSD and DIS, was finally captured by the 33rd Indian Infantry Brigade on 11 May, after a barrage of smoke shells blinded the Japanese machine-gun positions, thus allowing the troops to secure the hill and dig in.

The last Japanese positions on the ridge to be captured were the tennis court and gardens above the Deputy Commissioner's bungalow. On 13 May, after several failed attempts to outflank or storm the position, the British finally bulldozed a track to the summit above the position, up which a tank could be dragged. A Lee tank crashed down onto the tennis court, destroying the Japanese trenches and bunkers there. The 2nd Battalion, Dorsetshire Regiment, followed up and captured the hillside where the bungalow had once stood, finally clearing Kohima Ridge. Again, what was revealed to those there was enough to make even the most combat-hardened of veteran's vomit. The terrain was reduced to a fly-, maggot- and rat-infested wilderness, with half-buried human remains everywhere. The conditions under which the Japanese had lived and fought were described as 'unspeakable'. Gom Saipur, who was with the men of the 2nd Battalion Dorsetshire Regiment as they arrived on Kohima Ridge, recalled:

It was worse than any hell the Bible could have recorded. I saw parts of dead bodies sticking up out of the ground, and sometimes you would see a leg, or an arm; flies and maggots swarmed over these remains and rats scurried around feeding on the rotting flesh of the dead Japanese. There was also human excrement everywhere. The Japanese were never particular with their hygiene. They would defecate into the very holes where they were having to eat, sleep and fight. It was a miracle they were not all wiped out by disease alone in this hell. The smell was beyond description. How can I possibly describe what was truly beyond any description, so awful? What was worse was that some Japanese, driven mad by hunger, had even began to eat parts of the dead lying around on the battlefield. Yes, I saw injuries on corpses that were not made by bullets or shrapnel. These injuries were too neat, pieces of flesh sliced away with surgical precision. When captured Japanese were questioned, some admitted that they had turned to cannibalism purely to survive. It was quite the vilest practice, and I would rather have shot myself than turn to eating my own comrades' corpses.

The situation deteriorated further for the Japanese as yet more Allied reinforcements arrived. The 7th Indian Division, commanded by Major-General Frank Messervy, was arriving piecemeal by road and rail from the Arakan. Its 33rd Indian Brigade had already been released from XXXIII Corps reserve to join the fighting on Kohima Ridge on 4 May. The 114th Indian Infantry Brigade and the division headquarters arrived on 12 May, with 161st Brigade under command. The division concentrated on recapturing the Naga Village from the north. The independent 268th Indian Infantry Brigade was used to relieve the brigades of the British 2nd Division and allow them to rest before they resumed their drive southward along the Imphal Road.

However, when the Allies launched another attack on 16 May, the Japanese continued to stubbornly defend Naga Village and Aradura Spur. An attack on Naga Hill on the night of the 24/25 May gained no ground. Another attack mounted against both ends of the Aradura Spur on the night of 28/29 May was even more decisively repulsed by the Japanese defenders. The repeated setbacks, in combination with exhaustion, plus the effects of the climate all began to have a detrimental effect upon the morale of the British 2nd Division.

The decisive factor in the campaign from the Japanese perspective was that of supply. The Japanese as already mentioned began to forage or rather take what they wanted from local villages, where they were now far from welcome. Shortly before the siege of Kohima began the Japanese had captured a huge warehouse in Naga Village in which was stored enough rice to feed the entire Japanese division for three years. Unfortunately for the Japanese, the warehouse was bombed and the stock of rice totally destroyed. Other Japanese lines of supply were steadily severed. When supply opportunities did arise, the Japanese chose ammunition over food as opposed to a compromise between rations and ammunition. The Japanese forces slowly began to starve. They turned to feeding on captured Allied soldiers, and some were kept alive by the Japanese specially for this purpose. Where there were no Allied dead to take flesh from, they would take flesh from the corpses of their own dead.

The Indian XXXIII Corps was hot on the trail of the retreating Japanese. The British 2nd Division advanced down the main road, while the 7th Indian Division – using mules and Jeeps for most of its transport – moved through the rough terrain east of the road. On 22 June, the leading troops of the British 2nd Division met the main body of the 5th Indian Infantry Division advancing north from Imphal at Milestone 109, thirty miles south of Kohima. The siege of Imphal was now over, and truck convoys could now rapidly deploy vital heavy goods to the troops there.

During the Battle of Kohima, the British and Indian forces lost 4,064 men, killed, missing or wounded. Against this figure the Japanese lost 5,764 casualties in the fighting in the Kohima area, and many of the 31st Division subsequently died of disease, starvation or killed themselves. Never again would the Japanese taste victory in the Far East theatre; in all respects it was 'game over'. The demise of the Japanese in their war in the Far East was a painful one, marred by starvation, disease and the humiliation of retreat. They had begun their ambitions in the Far East as an all-conquering force yet were now reduced to what appeared a vagabond army that had fallen well short of the imperialist dream it had once aspired to. Worse retribution was yet to come and would fall upon the inhabitants of Hiroshima and Nagasaki. The battles of Imphal and Kohima, fought by a now largely forgotten army, effectively ended Japanese superiority in the Far East. It had been a close, tough and harrowing journey for the Allied forces, yet they had prevailed and prevailed brilliantly with great courage that should never be forgotten.

Two Victoria Crosses were awarded for actions during the Battle of Kohima. The first was to Lance-Corporal John Pennington Harman (29) 4th Battalion, Queen's Own Royal West Kent Regiment, 161st Indian Infantry Brigade, 5th Indian Infantry Division: 'During heavy fighting around "Detail Hill" [FSD?] during the siege, he single-handedly took out two Japanese machine gun posts, the first on 7/8 April and a second on 8/9 April. He was killed withdrawing from the second attack and subsequently posthumously awarded the Victoria Cross for these actions.' The second one was to Captain John Neil Randle, 2nd Battalion, Royal Norfolk Regiment, 4th Infantry British Infantry Division. Captain Randle's VC was awarded posthumously for his gallant action during the Kohima Battle. He was 26 years old.

Chapter 13

The Plight of the Japanese 'Comfort Women'

The term 'comfort women' where the Japanese forces in the Second World War were concerned is used merely in the derogatory sense. Many of the women procured for the purpose of providing the Japanese soldiers with 'comfort' were forced into doing so and did not give their bodies to this service willingly. In all of the territories conquered by the Japanese in the Second World War young girls and women were taken by force and abused, raped and assaulted by their Japanese captors at their leisure. Those who protested were either shot or bayoneted to death. Women with babies or young children were often forced to comply with their Japanese captors who often threatened to kill their children in retribution for any refusal. The Imperial Japanese Army had indulged in the sexual slavery of girls and young women prior to the outbreak of the Second World War, in China in particular. It is believed that the Japanese forced as many as 410,000 women of varying nationalities, including Chinese, Korean, Filipinos, Burmese, Malayans and Thais, into prostitution. A small number of European women from the Netherlands, Australia and Holland were also known to have been forced into prostitution by the Japanese. Naturally, Japanese historians argue against this figure, putting it more at around 20,000 female victims. Either way, these women were not prostitutes by trade. They were ordinary civilian women of the conquered territories specifically sought out by the Japanese forces to provide comfort to its army under the threat of execution. The arrogance of the Japanese regarding this issue is typified in the many personal photographs that Japanese soldiers took and often sent back home, photographs which depict them sexually torturing and abusing young women while strapped to chairs, trees or tables. One of the most disgusting of these images depicts a young

Chinese girl who had been bound to a chair in a way that she could be raped at will. Either side of her in the photograph Japanese troops kneel beside her helpless form wearing toothy smiles and giving thumbs-ups. Often the women were initially lured into prostitution by promises of work in factories or restaurants or promises of being given higher education to help their prospects in life. Once within the clutches of the Japanese, they were taken to special camps where they were incarcerated and forbidden to leave. These special camps were also set up abroad.

The Japanese argument regarding comfort women was that by having them, it would help prevent any occurrence of rape in the conquered territories, thus preventing hostility among the population. Sexual disease was also a serious issue in the IJA, and it was felt that instituting the policy of comfort women would minimize the threat posed by venereal diseases.

The origins of what the Japanese referred to as 'comfort stations' began in Shanghai in 1932. By the outbreak of the Second World War, prostitution in Japan had been organized into a very highly tuned machine. Staffed initially by Japanese women volunteers, the Japanese soon found that there were nowhere near enough volunteers to meet demand and therefore girls and young women of the local population were either coerced or abducted into the trade. Few were aware that they were being taken into sexual slavery for the pleasure of the Japanese military.

Stuart Hodgson, an Australian Second World War veteran who fought the Japanese in the steaming jungles of New Guinea, recalled:

> It was common knowledge that the Japanese took and held women of any nationality they encountered for sexual purposes. In New Guinea we encountered a few of the camps where women had been kept for the entertainment of Japanese troops. These facilities were far from what one might call clean. They were dirty, disgusting and filthy rat-infested huts built up from jungle foliage. The Japanese soldiers by their very nature, quite apart from their jungle lifestyle, were filthy dirty. You could smell a Jap from miles away; they stank of bodily odour – it was a smell unique to the Japanese.
>
> In the one camp which they had abandoned prior to our arrival there was a bamboo hut and inside we discovered the

bodies of what looked to be women of Asian origin. There were ten of them inside the hut, all of them were dead. It appeared that before the Japs left they killed them all by bayonet point. The hut was crawling with all manner of filth in the form of human excrement, urine, blood, maggots and flies. All the women were completely naked, and it was pretty obvious what they had been kept here for. We found numerous shallow graves containing the remains of babies. We guessed that these babies belonged to the women who had probably been made pregnant by their Japanese captors. The infants being of no use were either killed or thrown outside the huts where they were left to die. What surprises me most was how much of this was hushed up after the war. This kind of thing was going on all over Asia and the Pacific; it was barbarous.

An American friend of mine saw these kinds of Jap army brothels in the Pacific. The Japs had a thing for the young Philippine girls, and they were not particular about how young they were either. He told me he had been with US Marines who had liberated one such camp. Inside there were Filipino girls who looked barely 15 years of age. Most were in a dreadful state, not starving but unkempt with matted hair and marks all over their bodies. They told the Marines the Japanese would beat them before forcing them into having sex with them. It wasn't just sex though: they enjoyed inflicting pain and suffering on women. I'm not sure I should really go into the gory details as they are so depraved that people might not even believe it, but I will tell you. He told me some of these women had bamboo sticks inserted in their private parts and their breasts burned with cigarettes. One of the girls had her left nipple bitten completely off by one of the Japanese brutes. The wound had become swollen, red and infected with pus; it was a miracle she was still alive. The older female victims told him that if the soldiers couldn't penetrate a girl through the normal means they would force them the other way, through their anus. When I heard this, I wasn't surprised at all, I don't think any of us were. We had seen ourselves the violence that the Japanese were capable of and this was just an extension of their behaviour overall. They possessed a particular contempt, even loathing, for women apart from those of their own nationality it would seem. The native women who inhabited the jungles of Asia and the Pacific weren't spared either. The Japanese wiped out whole villages of indigenous peoples; they kept the women alive until last before they raped them and then killed them. Some were killed in a ritualistic fashion, staked to the ground in crucifix form where they were left at the mercy of wild animals or to die in the sun. They usually staked them to the ground in a clearing where there was no shade from the sun, and often soil was packed into their mouths to heighten their agony. It was in most respects better for a woman to shoot herself than fall into the captivity of the Japanese.

A typical story of how many young girls and women fell into the clutches of the Japanese and forced into sexual slavery is epitomized by the story of young Korean girl Lee Ok-Seon, who was 14 years old at the time. She recalled:

> I was running an errand at the time when a group of uniformed men burst out of a car, attacked me and dragged me into their vehicle. I had no idea at the time that I would never see my parents again. I was taken to what they called a 'comfort station', a brothel used by the Japanese soldiers. This station was in Japanese-occupied China and I was just one of thousands of other so called 'comfort women'. I was held a captive at this station where I was forced to have sex with Japanese soldiers. The conditions were inhumane, and we were not treated well by our captors and were subject to violence and brutality frequently. These places were no place for human beings. For many of the girls like myself there was no rest: they wanted sex all of the time.

Another now-elderly Korean woman recalled how Japanese soldiers searched people's homes for suitable young women to take to their comfort stations. Soo Ling Ka was 16 when the Japanese came. She recalled that fateful day.

> They came down our street, kicking in doors of houses and shouting for any women to come out. They weren't interested in the old women and would push them back into their homes. It was the young ones they were seeking. Parents would desperately attempt to hide their daughters from the soldiers. My mother and father tried to hide me inside a basket, but I was too tall to fit inside it and the soldiers found me. They beat both my parents for what they said was the crime of 'telling them lies'. I was slapped across the face, then they bound my hands and pushed me out of the door of my home into the street. My mother tried to plead with them, but they pointed their rifles at her, forcing her back into the house. A military truck came down the street and all of the young women that had been taken from their homes were forced at gunpoint to get into the back. There were soldiers in the back of this truck, so we had no way of jumping out to escape them.
>
> They drove us several miles into the jungle to a camp. When we arrived at this camp, we found the conditions terrible. There was nowhere proper to wash or for us to keep clean. It was also the first time that I had ever been away from my parents. If you cried or looked at them in the wrong way, they would beat you. When the soldiers came, all I can say is that it hurt, it was humiliating and painful. Once one had finished having sex with you, a different one would come in and force himself upon you. There was no escape and you could not refuse them sex. When they were not having sex with me, I had to sit and watch them force themselves on the other girls. We were all worried about contracting sexual diseases from these men. Most of them were dirty and they stank, their hygiene was very poor. There were women who fell pregnant from being forced into this sex slavery. Often the women miscarried due to the dreadful conditions and those babies that were carried for their full term were often taken away and killed

by the Japanese when they were born. Their savagery was shocking to me. I had heard all kinds of stories about them doing things but only when I saw them with my own eyes could I believe that men could behave like that. It is true, they would take babies and bayonet them, often playing games of cat and mouse with the infant by throwing it up into the air as one might a football. As the infant was thrown up, the soldiers would try to skewer it with their bayonets. They say this is all lies that it did not happen, yet it did happen, and I was not the only one to witness them doing these and other terrible things. I could not comprehend how someone could be so full of hatred, could be so void of compassion and so cruel as they were.

When we were freed, all I wanted to do was to go back home, to go and find my mother and father. When I finally found them, they barely recognized me I looked so bad. Because of what they did to me I was unable to have children myself; they did so much damage to our bodies and often gave us serious infections that would stay with us for years afterwards. When I heard of the two bombs that fell upon Hiroshima and Nagasaki, I felt no empathy for them, only joy. It has taken a great many years for me to be able to say I can forget what they did to me, but never can I forgive them.

Aung Lai-Chi was 17 when the Japanese approached her and told her that if she came and worked for them, she would be paid very well and looked after. They told her that she could work doing domestic things such as cleaning and doing washing for the soldiers. She recalls:

I was excited as they made their offer sound very good. It was only when I was taken to this place, a series of huts in the jungle, that I realized they had lied to me. I was one of the lucky ones. I managed to slip away from them and I ran out into the jungle. I knew the area well but even, so it took me a couple of days to find my way back home. Some other local villagers helped me to get back home. When I turned up my parents were furious; my father beat me and forbade me to even go outside for many months afterwards. He was terrified that the Japanese might come back for me, but they didn't. The fact that the Japanese were coercing young girls into their camps to imprison them for sex in the jungles of Burma was frightening to me. I was happy that it was not too long until the war was won, and they were gone. All the evidence was left behind in the jungle for our liberators to see for themselves. When I look back now, all these long years later, I understand how lucky I was. Many of the girls they took were killed or left to starve as the Japanese began to retreat. All that was left were these huts full of corpses. When these were cleared after the war, the locals refused to live in the area. They would say the angry ghosts of the dead haunted these places.

The saddest thing of all with these vile operations run by the Japanese was the fact that the end of the war did not bring an end to these brothels. In 2007 Associated Press reporters discovered that the United States authorities had allowed the continuity of these military brothels to operate well beyond the cessation of hostilities. It was discovered that tens of thousands of American men were guilty of using the services of these same women until Douglas Macarthur shut the operation down in 1946.

By then a figure was mooted that between 20,000 and 410,000 women had been enslaved in 125 brothels. In 1993, the United Nations Global Tribunal on Violations of Women's Human Rights estimated that by the end of the war, 90 per cent of the women procured into this vile sex slavery had died. At the end of the war, documents relating to Japanese sex slavery and the brothel system were destroyed by Japanese officials. The Japanese would not admit to any wrongdoing and effectively refused to acknowledge the pain and misery they had caused to thousands of innocent women. Therefore, many of the statistics quoted are those based on what little evidence remained for historians to examine.

As Japan began to rebuild at the end of the war, the story of how imperial Japan enslaved women was conveniently pushed to the back of Japanese consciousness. Those young women fortunate enough to have survived their sexual slavery, found themselves outcasts within their own society and many took their own lives, unable to live with the shame and stigma of what they had been through.

It was only as recently as the 1980s that many of the surviving comfort women came forward to tell their stories. They stand as a largely silent testimony to the levels of sadism perpetrated by the Japanese. Ninety-year-old Yong Soo Lee, one of those surviving victims, said of her suffering, 'I never wanted to give comfort to those men. Yet, I don't want to hate or hold a grudge, but I can never forgive them for what they did to me.'

Chapter 14

Humans Don't Taste Like Chicken

Akihara Koto was surprisingly frank when addressing my questions as to why Japanese troops turned to cannibalism in the Far East during the war. It had been a subject I was anxious to talk to him about, yet on previous occasions he had insisted he was not yet ready to discuss the issue. Fearing that he would never be in the right mood to address my questions on the subject, I had decided to abandon all hope of him ever talking about it. Yet, it was shortly before his death in April 2015 that I finally received an email with an attached file where he not only expressed his opinions but also his complicity in acts of cannibalism. It seemed that here was a man who found it easier to discuss his feelings with a 'screen' rather than face to face with another human being sitting before him. His opening words were remarkably frank, as follows:

They always say most things, most exotic meats taste like chicken. Humans don't taste like chicken, they tasted more like pork meat than they did chicken. When you have been fighting to near exhaustion in a jungle environment where food becomes virtually non-existent, you will yearn for anything solid with which to place between your lips and to fill that gnawing hole in your stomach. To be at the point of starvation is like no other pain in the universe. You can't sleep because of it; you have no energy to march and fight and your bowel ceases to function as you have not eaten anything. When we went into the jungle and we came upon villages, there would be pigs and chickens there; the villagers were not happy about you coming and taking their livestock, and often they were shot if they argued with us. We would then take their animals for food supplies, but between us the meat ration provided by these animals did not stretch far enough even with the rice ration we were allocated. I was telling my friend that I wished we had more meat, so we could eat better. We thought about the villagers we had killed earlier, and we just thought why should we not try some of their meat? When we went and examined the bodies of the villagers, it was obvious that the most tender parts of the body were the backs of the thighs and buttocks. We used a sharp knife and cut just a few small pieces from these areas of one of the bodies. The pieces of meat were then fried in a pan and we put this with some rice and sat down to eat it. What were my thoughts as I put the meat in my mouth and chewed it? It didn't taste like monkey, rat, snake or chicken – it tasted more like pork, just like pig meat. Some of the other soldiers of our unit came and sat with us and we offered them some of the meat. They ate it with some rice, and all agreed it tasted very good. They then went and cut more pieces from the bodies and fried it in the pan. Even one of our officers came and joined us. He made it very clear to us that eating parts of our own soldiers was strictly forbidden under all circumstances. Yet we were permitted to use parts of enemy dead rather than suffer the risk of starvation through lack of food supplies which became a problem for our army as the fighting progressed.

All I can say is that we had to do whatever we had to do to survive, to continue to fight for our emperor and our nation and the people of Japan. Things became so very bad in the jungle war. Supplies of food could not get through to us by air or by ground, especially by 1944. We would eat anything we could find – birds, spiders, snakes, insects, even pieces of foliage from the trees, we were that hungry at times. At night I lay there trying to sleep and thinking of the food I could be enjoying had I not been here in this jungle. I dreamed of bowls of steaming white rice and succulent fish with vegetables and pork soup, all the things we didn't have and were not likely to receive until this war was over. We were barely existing on a small ball of rice, sometimes for several days. Now do you see why the dead body of a human was sometimes consumed. It was a way out of the agony of raging hunger. When a body dies there is no soul trapped within; we felt no shame in using it to survive, just as many ancient tribes had done so throughout history. I knew some of my friends in my unit had also tried human meat – they had tried the testicles, liver, kidneys, even the heart.

Koto was keen to make the point that not all Japanese soldiers partook in the act of eating Allied war dead. He also made the point that the consumption of human flesh took on an almost spiritual significance. Either way I was not surprised when reading the contents of his narrative, yet it still filled me with disgust.

The following text was obtained from a captured Japanese order on the subject of cannibalism and the consumption of human flesh. Japanese officer Major Matoba was also interrogated on this subject by a military commission convened in August 1946 by the United States Navy commander of Guam and the Mariana Islands.

ORDER REGARDING EATING FLESH OF AMERICAN FLYERS

1. The battalion wants to eat the flesh of the American aviator Lieutenant (Junior Grade) Hall.
2. First Lieutenant Kanamuri will see to the rationing of this flesh.
3. Cadet Sakabe (Medical Corps) will attend the execution and have the liver and gall bladder removed.

Battalion Commander:	Major Matoba
Date:	9 March 1945
Time:	9 a.m.
Place:	Mikazuki Hill Headquarters
Method of issuing orders:	Called to my presence First Lieutenant Kanamuri and Cadet Sakabe and given verbal order
To report to after completion of order:	Brigade Commander – Major General Tachibana
Also informed:	Divisional Headquarters Detachment – Major Horie, 308 Independent Infantry Battalion

The US Military Commission asked Major Matoba to relate the circumstances around the first case of cannibalism of which he had personal knowledge. Matoba then gave the commission the following statement:

> The first case of cannibalism occurred between 23 and 25 February 1945. On that day I went to Divisional Headquarters and personally reported to General Tachibana that an American flyer would be executed at the Suyeyoshi Tai. While I was there sake was served, and the conversation turned to the Japanese forces stationed on Bougainville and New Guinea, and it was mentioned that the troops had been on very short rations and had had to eat human flesh. While I was still at the Divisional Headquarters a telephone call came through from 207 Infantry Battalion HQ asking us both to come over to a party which Colonel Kato had prepared for General Tachibana and myself. We walked to Colonel Kato's quarters and when we arrived, we found that he did not have enough 'eats' to go with the drinks. The General was annoyed, and a discussion took place as to where some meat and more sake could be obtained. The General then asked me about the execution, and possibility of getting some meat in that way. I therefore telephoned to my own headquarters and ordered them to send over some meat and sugarcane rum at once to 307 Battalion. The meat arrived and was cooked in Colonel Kato's room. It was human flesh. Everyone ate some of the flesh, but nobody relished the taste.

This particular event does not appear to have been a culinary success yet was nevertheless repeated on a number of other occasions. General Tachibana decided that this procedure should be adopted after every POW execution, and made these views known at one of his conferences. Painfully aware that supplies would diminish, and ammunition run short, he remarked that 'In the end the men would have to fight even with rocks and would be forced to eat even their own comrades killed in combat and also the flesh of their enemies'. Tachibana emphasized this point at more than one conference. On one occasion, when all his battalion commanders were present, he said: 'the invasion of the island is now imminent and it will probably be the last battle before the invasion of Japan itself.' He then reiterated once more 'that even when ammunition and food had run out the Japanese soldiers must still go on fighting and live off the flesh of their comrades and that of the enemy where circumstances dictated'. He was of the opinion that the Allied enemy were nothing more than 'beasts' and should be treated as such. In fact, Suzuki and Tojo were both guilty of using the same phrase when referring to Allied troops, yet it is doubtful as to whether or not they intended it to be so literally interpreted as it was by General Tachibana and his officers. Tachibana was by no means alone in his opinions on the consumption of human flesh, especially that of the Allied enemy. It would seem that the Japanese practice of cannibalizing the dead occurred chiefly in the New Guinea and Solomon Islands campaigns. And, as we have already heard in previous chapters, the Japanese had been actively eating human flesh in the Burma campaign.

It would seem that the practice of eating each other within the Japanese military never received official approval, for an order was issued on 10 December 1944 from Eighteenth Army HQ to the effect that while troops were permitted to eat the flesh of Allied dead, they must not eat their own. Furthermore, a memorandum on 'Discipline' found in the possession of a Japanese major general contained the following passage: 'Although it is not prescribed in the criminal code, those who eat human flesh (except that of the enemy), knowing it to be so, shall be sentenced to death as the worst kind of criminal against mankind.' Again, the consumption of enemy flesh was never considered a crime in Japanese military law. In many cases such a disgusting indulgence was turned into a festive occasion in the privacy of the officers' mess. Even admirals and generals took part in these festivities; the flesh of murdered Allied prisoners of war, or soup made from such flesh, was also served to the other ranks. There is substantial evidence that however meagre food supplies were for the Japanese, there were other food sources available, so it is likely that cannibalism was practised out of choice rather than necessity on many occasions.

Mark Rutherford backed up many of the reports of Japanese cannibalism in Malaya and Burma:

> Yes, I began to hear things; we all did. We began to hear news that filtered down from the officers about the Japs

killing locals and eating parts of their bodies. At first you think, 'Oh, come on, this has to be propaganda, surely?' But no, no it wasn't, and I think many of us had inadvertently witnessed it. A mate of mine had seen the bodies of women that the Japs had raped and then shot. There were the normal gunshot wounds, but then there were these other more peculiar wounds on their breasts and buttocks. The wounds were in the form of near-perfect squares: squares of flesh had been cut away almost to the bone and were missing. The pieces of flesh were not found; they were not discarded near any of the bodies. We could only assume from this that the Japs had taken the flesh for some reason. A Gurkha had killed one and when the Jap's body was searched, he discovered pieces of flesh wrapped up in jungle plant leaves. He told me that the skin was light with very fine hairs on, that it didn't look like the skin of an animal such as a pig or anything as it was too soft, too delicate. He was certain it was human flesh, yet the Japs weren't short on food at that time. They were fucking vile, that's all I can say. They defied all humanity when they started the war in the first place. When the stories of Japs eating our dead prisoners of war became frequent, we were not surprised. We were just more determined to beat the bastards and make them pay for it. I don't know how anyone could eat another human being's flesh. I think no, I'd rather starve to death than indignify myself in that way.

Tommie Watkins concurs:

We heard they used to cut the livers out of captured American pilots. They hated the American pilots with a passion, but to do that – cut a man open, take his innards and cook and eat them? – no, that is not the action of any normal human being, is it? I heard they sometimes took Allied prisoners and dissected them while they were still conscious, specifically to retrieve organs for their own consumption. They'd eat human flesh with their sake and rice. I'm sorry, but this all brings it back to me and it makes me angry, it makes me very bloody angry. It made the job of killing them very easy.

This was the first time I saw the normally jovial and placid Tommie get really angry. As he talked, he was like a man possessed for a few minutes, his eyes staring wide, his face red with rage, his fists clenched so tightly they turned white. It was if the events he was recounting had just happened yesterday, not seventy years ago. For a few minutes he sat quietly; tears began to well in his eyes as he said:

I'm sorry about that, Tim; but do you know so few paid the price for their criminal acts. A lot of those Japs got away with it. While the Allied powers were stretching the necks of high-profile Nazis, there were thousands of Japanese war criminals walking free who would never have to answer for their crimes. I don't understand why there were not more efforts made to bring them to justice for the horrors they perpetrated. I know I probably might be construed as being wrong in saying this, but I felt fucking sorry for the Germans. They've been persecuted ever since 1945 for the things they did; they paid a heavy price by having their country divided between east and west, one half under Stalin, another mass-murdering crook in my view. Yet look at Japan, look at how its prospered into a global manufacturing superpower. Yes, they were devastated by the two atom bombs, but I don't feel that they've ever been made to pay for what they did, not properly anyway.

Chapter 15

When a Sun of Silver Rose

It is 8.15 a.m., 6 August 1945. Above the Japanese city of Hiroshima a tiny silver speck indicates the presence of an aircraft flying at high altitude in the clear blue skies above. Some of the inhabitants gaze up at the speck in the sky yet show little concern. Most are going about their business as normal. A grandfather has just let his little granddaughter out into the back garden where she plays on a swing. At this moment the war and its failing fortunes appear a million miles away from Japan. In a few short seconds all of this will change as the bomb-bay doors open on the *Enola Gay*, a USAAF B-29 Superfortress bomber. The payload aboard *Enola Gay* is 'Little Boy', a uranium gun-type atomic bomb. As the bomb is released over the city and the 44.4 seconds to detonation count down, few can imagine that the history of warfare, and the world, is about to change forever. When the bomb detonates at a height of 1,968 feet above the city with a blast yield of fifteen kilotons of TNT, for those on the ground it is indeed as if the world has ended.

Shige Hiratsuka, a resident of Hiroshima, was a 29-year-old mother of two young children who gave an extremely harrowing account of the moment the bomb exploded over Hiroshima, its immediate aftermath and the horrific death of her 6-year-old daughter Kazuko who was trapped by debris and subsequently burned to death.

> It was a little after 8 a.m. I, my husband and our two children had just finished having our breakfast. I was washing up and cleaning the breakfast dishes and putting them away while my husband was sitting reading his newspaper. Our two children were playing nearby. In a split second there was what appeared to be a flash of lightning followed by this thunderous noise. Our home crashed down all around us, and we were all trapped. My husband and I managed to

free ourselves and as we looked around us, we could see there were nothing left of the city, just walls of flames all around us. My husband was quite badly injured, and he could barely move. In a panic I began looking around for our two children. I heard our 6-year-old daughter Kazuko crying out, 'Mummy, Mummy.' I shouted out, 'Where are you?' Kazuko cried out, 'I can't breathe.' When I found Kazuko, she was buried from the chest down in debris from the house. She continued to shout out, 'Mummy, get me out now' and 'Hurry Mummy.' I tried to pull her free with all my strength, but I could not free her. The fires by this time were moving closer to us. The flames were soon at our feet and all around us and it was becoming unbearably hot. Kazuko cried out, 'My leg is hurting me, I can't breathe.' I told her, 'I am a bad mother to you.' Kazuko shouted back, 'No, Mummy, don't go, don't go, it's too hot for me here.' I began to cry and I told her again, 'I am a bad mother to you, Kazuko.' She then began to scream out in pain, 'Ahhhh, it's hurting me.' I said to her, 'You don't want to die either, I know. Mummy is not brave enough to stay and die with you.' She continued to cry out, 'Mummy, where are you?' I shouted to her, 'Kazuko, forgive me' and these were my last words to my little daughter. Her last cries were, 'The fire is burning me.' There was an agonized scream then she went quiet. I knew then my daughter was gone. She was dead.

An elderly grandfather who had just seconds ago allowed his granddaughter into the garden to play rushed outside in the aftermath of the blast to find a curious black silhouette on the ground. This was all that was left of the little girl, who had been vaporized in the blast.

These are typical accounts of the Hiroshima bombing from those who had witnessed it. They are like so many and each make horrific and disturbing reading. The Japanese at the time had no idea of what had just hit them.

On 9 August 1945, a second bomb was dropped, on the city of Nagasaki. This was the 'Fat Man' bomb, a plutonium implosion atomic bomb delivered by a USAAF B-29 Superfortress bomber named *Bockscar*.

At this point the reader may well be asking what relevance does all this have to the jungle war in Asia. The simplest answer to the question is to ask the veterans themselves. Tommie Watkins:

> Were the two atom bombs dropped on Japan out of proportion from a military point of view? Not at all – they were entirely justified when you look at the sheer scale of criminality of the whole Imperial Japanese regime: the barbarism the Japanese were responsible for, all the horrors perpetrated against Allied prisoners of war. For example, the Burma Railway, where for every sleeper laid down an Allied prisoner of war died – that's a hell of a lot of deaths in its entirety. Yes, the atomic bombs killed a lot of civilians, but then the Japanese military would have never given up the fight had it not been for those two atomic bombs. Do I feel sorry for them? No, I don't feel sorry for the Japanese and the way they were bombed into surrender. They were waging an aggressive, expansionist war in the Far East, and they did unspeakable things in the execution of their war. If the atomic bombs had not been used then we would have lost thousands upon thousands of more Allied soldiers, maybe even millions. It would have been too dreadful to comprehend having to invade mainland Japan knowing how the Japanese would have fought against us in an invasion. No, I'm afraid I agreed wholeheartedly with the use of the atomic bombs on Hiroshima and Nagasaki – they got what they deserved there. If anyone is to blame for those two bombs maybe the people of Japan should focus their anger against their emperor and their military rulers. They had the opportunity to surrender to avoid that horror, but no, they wanted to fight on: it was their decision not ours. It was their government and their emperor to blame – no one else.

Ron Rastal:

> I remember when the news broke that the Japs had given up and surrendered after these new bombs were used against Hiroshima and Nagasaki. At that time, we didn't

really know too much about the bombs, other than they were a completely new form of weapon with the power to raze whole cities to the ground. When we received the news, we were elated about it. Did I care that thousands of Japanese civilians had been wiped out? No, sorry, I didn't. I was just glad the war was now over, and we had survived it. Those two atomic bombs for us meant survival; we wouldn't have to go and probably die on Japanese home soil. That was always at the backs of our minds. We knew they'd fall back, but surrender? no, we couldn't ever imagine the Japs doing that. So, I thank the powers that be for creating a weapon that brought them to their knees and meant that we could go back home to our families, because a great many would never have experienced that had we had to invade Japan itself.

Flying Officer Michael Read Wright:

The atomic bomb was created under great secrecy. No one knew anything about them until they were unleashed on the Japanese cities of Hiroshima and Nagasaki. When we heard about those two cities literally being wiped off the map, we wondered what the hell type of bomb could do that much damage. Nothing in our conventional arsenal had that much power; not even the biggest of the 'Tall-Boy' bombs could wipe out a whole city. We guessed this was something very new and revolutionary and that we would learn more over the coming days and weeks about it. But we were so happy to get the news that Japan had surrendered; it was like Christmas Day for us, and we certainly had a very big celebration to mark the event, despite the thousands of dead and wounded in Hiroshima and Nagasaki. Japan paid a very heavy price, but it was entirely within proportion when one considers her crimes during the Second World War. Everywhere they went they raped, butchered and murdered and behaved in a totally undisciplined manner. Their leadership was arrogant and vain, and the atomic bombs were the biggest stick one could hit them with and hit them we did.

Robert McGilling:

> If I could have volunteered to have been aboard the *Enola Gay* on that historic flight to Hiroshima I would have gladly gone. Japan had spared no thought for the people of Russia, China, Burma, Borneo, India and all those places they were active in the Pacific. They were out and out brutes. I feel sorry for the many innocent and the children killed at Hiroshima and Nagasaki, but the Japanese spared no thought for the women and children whose lives they were responsible for taking. Japan was an aggressive nation and they would not have stopped fighting had they not been hit with these two highly controversial weapons. It not only signalled the end for Japan's imperialist desires but anyone else who had the same ideas as what they did.

Jaspal Singh sat quietly for some minutes before giving the following answer:

> Hiroshima and Nagasaki were two terrible events. As a young man I had been raised by my parents to cherish all living things, that we were all a part of one universe of humanity. It is difficult now for me to look back and be vengeful, with a heart full of hatred for the Japanese. I remember when we were told the war was over, about these new bombs the Americans had been developing. I thought it was remarkable that just two bombs could bring Japan to its knees. Japan had been bombed by the Allied air force countless times with no real effect. I wondered what had made these two bombs so different. They later revealed that the two bombs were atom bombs, the most powerful bombs then in existence, destroyers of worlds as their creator had called them. I didn't quite grasp how they worked at the time as nuclear physics was not something I had much knowledge of, being a simple countryman. After the war I read about them and how they worked and then I wondered what it must have been like in Hiroshima or Nagasaki when the bombs exploded. It must have been terrible. But had

those bombs not been used, more of us may have died in the fighting as it went on. Sadly, it was probably the only option left to make Japan surrender and even then, it took a second bomb to break their will.

Mark Rutherford has no such reservations:

I'd have gladly pressed the bomb release button myself. The Japs deserved all they got – they started it and we finished it. They were beyond the description of beasts; their mentality meant that only the severest of measures would have been effective against them. They were determined to fight on at all costs. Well, those two bombs soon stopped them, didn't they? We cheered for all we were worth when he received the surrender news. I for one didn't give a fuck how many Japanese civilians had perished in the two atomic bomb attacks. I'm pretty sure if they had refused to surrender after Nagasaki, we would have hit them again and again with more of these bombs until Japan was wiped from the map of the world. It was either that or send millions of men to their deaths to try and take their homeland. Make no mistake, they would have fought on had those two bombs not been used. You can't be sentimental in times of war. If you can knock out your enemy with a single blow then you do it; you fight a war to win it, not to lose it and we won it thanks to many men giving their lives and those two bombs. I don't look back and feel sorry for them [the Japanese]. I didn't like them then and I don't like them now – sorry if that sounds harsh but far too many of them got away with murder for me to feel any compassion for them especially that Hirohito: he should have been hanged as war criminal. If he had been this divine entity that the Japanese nation revered as some sort of god, then he should have steered the people away from war. His word surely would have counted for something over the military government, yet he did nothing to stop his country's aggression. As supreme ruler he did nothing to prevent Japanese aggression. It's a shame he wasn't in Hiroshima when that bomb went off.

Jaspal Gahor:

> I heard that many Japanese lay dead or wounded in Hiroshima and Nagasaki. Houses had been blown down like matchwood; these bombs were like no others ever used or witnessed by mankind at that time. These were called atom bombs and used uranium to generate their explosive power. They said the sky above Hiroshima became blinding, a light many times greater than that of the midday sun, with heat and fire that left no trace of human beings, a shockwave that flattened everything in its path then drew all that destruction back in as if a hand clawing its victims into the depths of hell itself. It all sounded very terrifying to me. Yet the war was over and that is what mattered at the time. I could go back home and begin life with my family once again, and carry on farming as my family had done for generations. We were the mountain people of Nepal. We were humble, god-fearing people that felt for all living things on the earth. Japan was defeated and I was happy they had been beaten. It was time to forget the war, forget the fighting; it was time to go home and time to become human once again. I hadn't felt human for a very long time: war makes you feel like that.

The Japanese perspective on Hiroshima and Nagasaki were understandably different from their western enemy. Akihara Koto:

> Those two terrible bombs were weapons from hell. When I heard that Hiroshima had been razed to the ground by a terrible new weapon, I initially thought it was propaganda to make us fight with a greater tenacity. We were not doing well at all and I honestly thought it was propaganda to spur us on, to make us full of rage. Days later Nagasaki was bombed with this new weapon and it too was razed to the ground. Then the news that we were surrendering came through. I couldn't believe that this could happen. We were prepared to fight on and to the death for our country and emperor if necessary. It was a heavy blow to us all, but we

soon learned that we had no answer militarily to this new weapon. If our forces did not surrender, then we would be attacked again. Later we learned that these new bombs were not like conventional ones. These bombs while not exactly huge were capable of destroying entire cities. They called them atomic bombs and these had been in development for many years in total secrecy. As time went by, we began to understand the mechanics of these weapons and most frightening was the fact that they emitted very high levels of deadly radiation. There were those who had survived the blast but would die in the days, weeks, months, even years after due to radiation poisoning. People were trying to bathe their wounds in water heavily contaminated with radiation; they also drank this contaminated water. Radiation poisoning meant a long, slow, painful death.

It was at this point I remarked on the long, slow, lingering deaths that many Allied prisoners of war had suffered at the hands of the Japanese, those men who were slowly worked and starved to death, denied basic food and medicine that may have saved their lives and beaten so badly they could barely even stand.

Akihara Koto sat with his head hung for some minutes as if trying to contemplate an answer to my question for which there was no answer. He sat shaking his head and then got up from his chair and walked off. He refused to talk again, reminding me that he was just an ordinary soldier who followed orders and that he had nothing further to tell me. It was certainly one of those rare, strange if tense, moments, few of which I have ever experienced previously in my interviews with war veterans.

Hikokuru Ishimaru had a rather more philosophical view when asked about the two atomic bombs used against his country:

It was simple for us: our gods, the gods that we had once revered and felt would give us their divine protection had abandoned us. The Japanese people were being punished. The new weapons being used against our cities were ones we could not equal. We had to accept defeat, however hard we knew it was going to be. We would surrender our swords, our honour, our pride. Thenceforth, we would go forward over the hot coals of our defeat – we would live and regain our lives. We understood that was the only way' there was no other way. When the order to surrender was transmitted to us, five of my friends took their swords and killed themselves in the traditional way of the Japanese warrior. I contemplated the same fate. I grasped the blade of my sword and placed it against my stomach – all I had to do was fall upon it and it would all be over. I could not do it; I threw down the sword and I wept with frustration. These two new bombs, what were they? How could they be so great to force us to surrender to our enemies? Later we saw the destruction of Hiroshima and Nagasaki and learned of these new bombs our enemy possessed. No warrior could have fought on against those. I drew comfort from that and I returned home to my family. I was not received as a coward by my mother and father: they were happy that I was not dead, and they were happy that the war was over. We understood that now we would have to reconcile with our former enemies.

Over the years since the end of the Second World War, many have questioned whether the use of the two atomic bombs against Japan was a rightful course of action. Many historians will agree that despite the horrific nature of these weapons, they were the vital big stick in forcing the Japanese to surrender, thus saving hundreds of thousands, if not millions, more lives. As many of the veterans of the Far East and Pacific theatres have concurred, the mere thought at having to mount a full-scale invasion of the Japanese mainland filled them with dread. Had such an operation been necessary, it is without doubt that the cost in human lives would have been astronomical. The two atomic bombs dropped on Japan, however terrible they may have been, were pivotal in bringing the Second World War to an end. They were also instrumental in maintaining an uneasy peace between the nuclear superpowers of east and west in the years following the end of war. Hiroshima and Nagasaki are the only victims of nuclear weapons in an armed conflict. One can only hope that they remain so.

When I last spoke with Ron Rastal, he reminded me that despite the Japanese surrender there were still small pockets of Japanese resistance that had to be dealt with in the jungles of the Far East. On this he recalled:

> There were some Japanese who refused to surrender even when ordered by their commanders to do so. I just thought, fucking hell here we go again: we are going to have to go after these little bastards and more of us will get killed in the process. I wasn't happy about it at all, but we had the Gurkhas with us. There was this Gurkha sergeant that I became friendly with. He was a man who feared nothing. We were conducting a patrol near an abandoned village in Burma one afternoon when there was this Jap up in a tree shouting at us, then he fired his rifle at us. Luckily, he didn't hit any of our patrol. The Jap was only really a lad with no experience; had he kept still, he could have killed one or more of us as we had no idea he was there until he started shouting then firing. One of our Japanese-speaking men shouted to him, 'The war is over; your country has surrendered. Throw down your arms and you can have food and water and go back home.' The young Jap replied with several more shots, probably until he ran out of ammunition. Our sharpshooter, a chap they nicknamed Jesse James because his surname was James, was a great shot. He took aim and shot the Jap through the shoulder. He could have blown his head off, but he didn't. The Jap fell out of the tree and ended up in a heap on the ground; we dived on him checked he had no hidden weapons and then treated the wound. Jessie just said, 'Well, this little cunt will be going home. I hope he will look back on this someday and appreciate it.' This Gurkha sergeant laughed and made this funny remark – well, I thought it was bloody funny. He clipped this young Jap around his ears and said, 'What a fine pair of ears I almost had!' We had a right laugh about that, and it still makes me laugh today when I think of it.

To round off this chapter, I feel the words of Chi Wong, the 8-year-old Chinese girl who survived the horrific events at Nanking, are most appropriate. Chi Wong had spoken frequently over the years with her grandson Huang and it was he who documented his grandmother's words for future generations. Huang very kindly granted me permission to use the following piece that his grandmother had written on the Japanese, and the two atomic bombs dropped on Japan in 1945.

I could feel no pity for them [the Japanese]. As the smoke and dust cleared, I learned of mothers desperately searching for their children, just as Chinese mothers had searched for theirs after Nanking. The mothers of Hiroshima and Nagasaki did not emerge from the smoke and dust to find their babies and little children impaled on bamboo spikes or beheaded by Samurai swords as many Chinese mothers had. Nor had they had to wipe the blood from between the thighs of their little daughters raped or sodomized by the Japanese soldiers. Their end [the Japanese mothers] was mercifully quick, for some they died within seconds of the blast, vapourized by a light brighter than a thousand suns. No, there is no pity and there can be no forgiveness in my heart for what they did to us and our people. They say the bombs were cruel, that people even today are suffering from the effects of radiation exposure. Yet, this is their penance, the cross they must bear for the evils of their leaders and in some cases their personal support of their leaders. No, I cannot find the power within my heart to forgive them for what they did to us. I am happy they suffered as we had once suffered, that they felt sorrow as we had once felt sorrow, and that they felt pain as we had once felt pain. The devil we were taught resides within the realms of fire, and the devil can be destroyed by that same fire, the fire of righteousness. When we read of the atomic attacks on Hiroshima and Nagasaki and we saw the photographs of the devastation wrought, we were happy. We knew from that day on they could never hurt our people again, from that I felt a sense of joy in my heart. There were no tears for the Japanese in China, only elation at their destruction and humiliation before the whole world.

Chapter 16

Retribution

In the wake of the dropping of the two atomic bombs on Japan, events which accelerated its defeat and subsequent surrender, the issue of war crimes had already been considered by the Allied powers. Despite the gravity of Japanese war crimes which occurred in every theatre where the Japanese were active, when compared to the Nuremberg trials, surprisingly few Japanese soldiers actually stood trial for their crimes. Thousands of Japanese soldiers literally got away with murder, including Emperor Hirohito himself, who should have been tried and punished as a war criminal. Many viewed Hirohito escaping the noose and retaining his godly status as the biggest insult of all to those who either lost their lives or were permanently crippled as a result of their treatment at the hands of Japanese barbarism in the Far East and Pacific.

On 24 August 1945, the day after the Japanese capitulation, the Chinese ambassador, as chairman of the Far-Eastern sub-committee at the United Nations War Crimes Commission (UNWCC), submitted a recommendation to the commission for the formation of an International Military Tribunal for the trial of Japanese responsible for criminal policies. Also recommended were the establishment of a Central War Crimes Agency in Japan to collect evidence and register war criminals, the setting up of a War Crimes Prosecuting Office, and the making of arrangements for the surrender of war criminals to the countries that had charged them. These recommendations were approved and the International Military Tribunal for the Far East, on which eleven nations were represented, was established by virtue of a special proclamation by General MacArthur on 19 January 1946.

Twenty-eight accused were brought before the tribunal upon an indictment containing fifty-five counts alleging crimes against peace, conventional war crimes, and crimes against humanity between 1 January 1928 and 2 September 1945. With the opening of the trial in Tokyo on 3 May 1946, the Declaration of Potsdam with regard to Japanese war criminals was implemented. This declaration had been made by the President of the United States of America, the President of the National Government of China, and the Prime Minister of Great Britain, and it was later adhered to by the USSR. It stated, among other things, that although the Allies did not intend that the Japanese people should be enslaved as a race or destroyed as a nation, stern justice should be served to all those found guilty of committing acts of war crime, including those who had visited cruelty upon Allied prisoners of war.

On 3 and 4 May 1946 the lengthy indictment was read in open court in the presence of all the accused, and the tribunal then adjourned until 6 May to receive their pleas. Incidentally, all of those accused pleaded not guilty to the charges they were facing. The tribunal was then fixed for 3 June for the opening of the case for the prosecution. In many cases the evidence was quite overwhelming. Again, in a reflection of the arrogance of the Japanese military, many had openly boasted of their heinous activities during their service. Some had even gone as far as to take photographs illustrating their deeds, seemingly proud of their exploits like hunters posing with their trophies.

The trial proved to be something of a marathon. The prosecution's case was duly opened on 3 June 1946 and closed on 24 February 1947. The presentation of evidence for the defence went on for eleven months, the trial finally ending in November 1948. Two of the Japanese accused brought before the tribunal and charged on the opening day, died during the course of the trial. A third was declared unfit to stand trial as he was unable to defend himself.

Of all the characters of this bazaar of brutality, the most notable war criminal was Hideki Tojo.

From 1937, when he was the Chief of Staff of the Kwantung Army, he was in close association with those Japanese, and particularly the military faction, planning the domination of China, East Asia and the Pacific. Tojo had also made plans for an attack on the USSR and an extension of Japanese military operations in China. Early in 1938 he vacated active command and became Vice-Minister of War before becoming Minister of War in July 1940. Appointed Prime Minister in October 1941, Tojo formed a cabinet and continued in office for almost three years. His part in the incidents which preceded the attack on Pearl Harbor is also well documented. The tribunal found that he bore major responsibility for Japan's criminal attacks on its neighbours. His responsibility for the maltreatment of prisoners of war and civilian internees was summed up by the tribunal in the following words:

> The barbarous treatment of prisoners and internees was well known to Tojo. He took no adequate steps to punish offenders and to prevent the commission of similar offences in the future.
>
> His attitude towards the Bataan Death March gives key to his conduct towards these captives. He knew in 1942 something of the conditions of that march and that many prisoners had died as a result of the conditions they experienced and brutal treatment by the Japanese. He did not call for a report on the incident. When in the Philippines in 1943 he made perfunctory inquiries about the march but chose to take no action. No one was punished.
>
> His explanation is that the commander of a Japanese army in the field is given a mission in the performance of which he is not subject to specific orders from Tokyo.
>
> Thus, the head of the Government of Japan knowingly and wilfully refused to perform the duty which lay upon that government of enforcing performance of the laws of war.
>
> To cite another outstanding example. He advised that prisoners of war should be used in the construction of the Burma–Siam Railway, designed for strategic purposes. He made no proper arrangements for billeting and feeding the prisoners, or for caring for those who became sick in that trying climate. He learned of the poor condition of the prisoners employed on the project and sent an officer to investigate. We know the dreadful conditions which that investigator must have found in the many jungle camps along the railway. The only step taken as a result of the investigation was the trial of one company commander for the ill-treatment of prisoners.
>
> Nothing was done to improve conditions. Deficiency diseases and starvation continued to kill off the prisoners until the end of the project. Statistics relative to the high death rate from malnutrition and other causes in prisoner

of war camps were discussed at a conference over which Tojo presided.

The shocking condition of the prisoners in 1944, when Tojo's cabinet fell, and the enormous number who had died from lack of food and medicine, is conclusive proof that Tojo took no proper steps to care for them.

We have referred to the attitude of the Japanese Army towards the Chinese prisoners of war. Since the Japanese government did not recognize the 'incident' as war, it was argued that the rules of war did not apply to the fighting and that Chinese captives were not entitled to the status and rights of prisoners of war. Tojo knew and did not disapprove of that shocking attitude.

He bears responsibility, also for the instruction that prisoners who did not work should not eat. We have no doubt that this repeated insistence on this instruction conduced in large measure to the sick and wounded being driven to work, and to the suffering and deaths which inevitably resulted.

It was no surprise that after such a judgement the tribunal sentenced Tojo to death by hanging. However, the attitude adopted by Tojo was endemic throughout all ranks in the Imperial Japanese Army. The most noteworthy Japanese war criminals in the Far East theatre of war are as follows:

Hiroshi Abe (born c.1922) served as a first lieutenant in the Imperial Japanese Army during the Second World War. Abe was responsible for overseeing the construction of the infamous Burma Railway at Songkrai. Over 12,000 Allied prisoners of war died under Abe's supervision. He was sentenced to death by hanging as a Class B/C class war criminal and imprisoned in Changi Prison. In 1948 his sentence was commuted to fifteen years. He was released in 1957. Unlike many, Abe was a repentant war criminal and once remarked, 'The construction of the railway was in itself a war crime. For my part in it, I am a war criminal.'

Tomoyuki Yamashita (born 8 November 1885) was the infamous IJA general nicknamed 'The Tiger of Malaya' and 'The Beast of Bataan'. Conqueror of Malaya and Singapore, his involvement in the Far East campaign was relatively short as he was then appointed to defend the Philippines. No evidence was found to suggest that Yamashita was complicit in the acts of barbarism perpetrated by the Japanese forces under his control, or that he approved or even knew of them. Nevertheless, he made no such efforts to prevent the rape, torture and murder of both civilians and Allied combatants during his tenure and was found guilty of war crimes. Aged 60, he was hanged at Los Banos, Laguna in the Philippines on 23 February 1946.

Heitarō Kimura (born 28 September 1888) was a general in the IJA. He was convicted of war crimes as commander of the Burma Area Army and hanged in Sugamo Prison, Tokyo, on 23 December 1948, aged 60.

Renya Mutaguchi (born 7 October 1888) was a lieutenant general in the IJA and field commander of Japanese forces during the Battle of Imphal. At the end of the war Mutaguchi was arrested by the American Occupation Authorities where he was then subjected to extradition to Singapore where he stood trial for war crimes. He was subsequently imprisoned but released in March 1948. He died in Tokyo on 2 August 1966.

The fact is a huge number of Japanese military personnel were guilty of war crimes yet never stood trial for their crimes. They returned home to their families and drifted back into peacetime obscurity. It seems a travesty of justice when even today – 2019 – elderly German war criminals are still actively pursued and prosecuted for their deeds while Japanese war criminals have no such concerns of being tracked down. Why is this? What makes a Japanese war criminal any different from any other? I believe the answers to these questions have both political and economic foundation which lie with the Allied powers who defeated Japan. One should not seek to blame the new generation of Japanese society for the deeds perpetrated by their forebears. Yet one should also not forget. We owe that to not only those who lost their lives in the war in the Far East but also those who came home as changed men, many of whom today feel that they have been largely forgotten by the country they were once prepared to trade their lives for.

Afterword

'When you go home
don't worry about what to tell your loved ones and friends
about service in Asia.
No one will know where you were, or where it is if you do.
You are and will remain "The Forgotten Army."'

The contents of this book represent one very small component within what was a very substantial machine. It would have been impossible to have covered every single action, event or aspect and remain within the permitted parameters of this volume. Yet I hope by the time the reader has reached this point in the book, he or she will have a better understanding of the unique privations, hardships and dangers those brave individuals of the Fourteenth Army faced in the jungles of the Far East in the Second World War. The Japanese enemy they had faced were truly unique in their brutality and savagery. This, combined with having to adapt to an environment many could only best describe as totally alien, meant their war was indeed unique in comparison to the one being fought in Europe itself. Void of urban sprawl, green fields and predictable seasons, the jungles of the Far East were dark, hot and humid, with danger seemingly lurking behind every bush. I recall a couple of friends who travelled to Burma back in 1999 with the intention of walking a good part of a well-trodden local jungle track. Both were hardened ex-soldiers, fit and well prepared for the trip. Barely a day into their hike, they were forced to retreat to their air-conditioned hostel as beaten men. Both, while physically and mentally prepared, had underestimated the sweltering heat and humidity of the jungle, though both gained a sliver of experience of what it must have been like to have had to live and fight in that environment as the men of the Fourteenth Army had done some fifty-four years before and in the same 50°C temperatures.

AFTERWORD

It is sad that some of the veterans I interviewed during the formulation of this book have since died. It was also a considerable blow when two of my contributors passed away within a short time of one another halfway through the project. The men who fought in these battles so long ago are now well into their twilight years. For some their memories remain as sharp and as vivid as if the events they experienced happened just yesterday. For others old age has not been so kind and their memories are now lost forever. Then there are those who find the prospect of talking about their experiences, even to historians with all good intent, just too unbearable and thus will never speak. This is something we have to both understand and respect and something I have encountered on more than a few occasions over the years.

Today books such as those I have spent twenty-six years researching are received with mixed reaction. There are those who fully understand how difficult a task it is to research and write something new in a historical context. My view years ago was if the information or data I was searching for was not there in the public domain, museums or archives, then I would have to go out and do the research and find it myself. This was something I enjoyed doing very much and never found it a chore despite it taking up virtually every minute of my spare time. It involved getting up early on a weekend after a hard week at work and catching trains all over the country in order to meet up and document the stories of war veterans. In that sense you are at times writing the textbook, the best example of this being my first book *Hitler's Girls: Doves Among Eagles*, even though that particular book came about quite by accident.

None of us are 'experts' as one can't possibly know everything and pieces of new history of which we were previously unaware are being discovered all the time with the technology we possess today. In many cases the truth is far more fantastic and difficult to believe than the fiction. This book, while far from extensive in its scope, has proved to be one of the most challenging I have written.

I hope it in some small measure provides something of a tribute, not only to those who have contributed to it, but to all the surviving veterans of the Fourteenth Army. I would like to think that today the Fourteenth Army is no longer the forgotten army it was yesterday.

Appendix

Notes on Japanese

It might be of some use to historians to include some information on interrogation narratives as conducted by the Allied forces questioning Japanese prisoners of war. The following shows typical interrogation questions followed by their Japanese equivalents.

What is your name? *Namae wa nan desu ka?*
What is your number? *Bango wa nan desu ka?*
What is your rank? *Kaikyu wa nan desuka?*
What is your arm of service?   *Heika wa nan desuka?*
What is your unit? Its number? *Shozoku butai wan a desu ka? Nan ban desu ka?*
What is your unit commander's name? *Butai cho no namae wa nan desu ka?*
Where is your unit now? *Butai wa ima doko desu ka?*
Where is Regiment, Battalion Headquarters? *(Rentai), (Daitai), Hombu wa doko desu ka?*
Where is Division, Divisional Infantry Headquarters? *(Shidan), (Hohei-Dan) shirei-bu wa doko desu ka?*
Point it out on this map (or sketch it). *Kono (chizu) (yozu) de shi-meshite kure.*
Draw a sketch map of ... *No yozu wo kaite kure ...*
Show me the position of ... *No ichi wo shimeshi te kure ...*
In what direction from here? *Doko no ho desu ka?*
Where is the unit marching to? *Butai wa doko e yuku ka?*
Where have you come from today? *Kyo doko kara kita ka?*
What is the strength of your unit? *Butai no heiryoku wa?*
What is your unit's task? *Butai no nimmu wa nan desu ka?*
What units are on your (right), (left) flank? *(Migi no), (Hidari no) Butai wan ani butai desu ka?*
Which are the (forward), (reserve) units? *Dai issen (no butai) (yobi tai) wan ani butai desu ka?*

Notes

The 'U' at the end of 'Masu' and 'Desu' is silent: pronounce as 'Mas' and 'Des'. 'Hei' is pronounced like 'Hay' not like 'High'. The 'U' of 'Kure' is pronounced like 'Fully' not like 'Cure' or 'Curry'. The 'I' of 'Shi' is short as in 'Bit' and not long as in 'Shy'. For unit/Butai substitute Regiment/Rentai, Battalion/ Daitai. Company/Chutai and Platoon/Shotai.

The following is a list of some typical Japanese phrases:

Cease fire!	*Uchikata yame!*
Halt!	*Tomare!*
Don't move!	*Ugokuna!*
Come closer!	*Motto chikazuke!*
Turn around!	*Maware migi!*
About turn!	*Ushiro muke!*
If you resist you will be shot!	*Teiko suru to utsu zo!*
Silence!	*Damare!*
Quick march!	*Susume!*
Put down your arms!	*Buki wo sutero!*
Take off your belt!	*Obikawa wo tore!*
Take off your hat!	*Boshi wo nuge!*
Take off your equipment!	*Sogu wo toke!*
Take off your loincloth!	*Fundoshi wo tore!*
Hand over your documents	*Shorui wo yokose!*
Hand over identity disc	*Ninshikihyo wo yokose!*
Don't lie!	*Uso wo tsukuna!*
Rifle	*Shoju*
Machine gun (light)	*Kei-kikanju*
Machine gun (heavy)	*Ju -kikanju*
Grenade	*Tekidan*
Grenade discharger	*Tekidan-to*
Grenade, hand	*Teryudan*
Gas	*Gasu*
Bomb	*Bakudan*
Landmine	*Jirai*
Anti-tank gun (quick firing)	*Sokusha-ho*
Battalion gun	*Daitai-ho*

Regiment gun	*Rentai-ho*
Field gun	*Yaho*
Mountain gun	*Sampo*
Mortar	*Kyuro*
Motor	*Jidosha*
Plane	*Hikoki*
Molotov cocktail	*Kaen-bin*
Attack	*Kogeki*
Defence	*Bogyo*
Advance	*Zenshin*
Retreat	*Taikyaku*
Capture (position)	*Senryo*
Position	*Jinchi*
Trench	*Zango*
Advance guard	*Zen-ei*
Main body	*Hontai*
Rear guard	*Koei*
Occupation of position	*Jinchisenryo*
Right	*Migi*
Left	*Hidari*

Acknowledgements & Sources

I would like to thank all the contributors to this work without whom this particular volume would not have been possible. Special thanks to Chris Cocks, not only for his work on the copy-editing of this book but also for his valued advice throughout its production. I would also like to offer thanks to the following institutions for their assistance with the provision of information and data for this work:

The Burma Star Association
The Department of Printed Books, The Imperial War Museum, Lambeth, London
The Far East Veterans' Association
The Japanese Embassy, 101–104 Piccadilly, Mayfair, London
The National Archives, Kew, Richmond, Surrey
The Royal Air Force Personnel Management Agency (RAF PMA)
The Zero Fighters Association (Japan). This former Zero fighter pilots' association is no longer in existence. The last contact I had with this organization was in 1994.

The following works were consulted throughout the writing of this book to ensure wherever possible clarification and accuracy with the facts:

Cross, J.P., *Jungle Warfare*, Guild Publishing, 1989
Edwards, Jack, *Banzai you Bastards*, Souvenir Press Ltd., 1991
Lord Russell of Liverpool CBE, MC, *The Knights of Bushido: A Short History of Japanese War Crimes*, Chivers Press, 1989
Slim, William, 1st Viscount Slim, *Defeat into Victory*, Cassell, 1956
Spencer Chapman DSO, F., *The Jungle is Neutral*, Chatto & Windus, 1949
Swinson, Arthur, *Defeat in Malaya: The Fall of Singapore*, MacDonald & Co., 1970
Zich, Arthur, *The Rising Sun*, Time-Life Books, 1977